T0165273

I'm Gonna Freaking Recover...
Am I?

**A personal look into one woman's recovery
from an eating disorder and depression**

By Sharon Cameron

iUniverse, Inc.
New York   Bloomington

I'm Gonna Freaking Recover...Am I?
A Personal Look into One Woman's Recovery from an Eating Disorder and Depression

Copyright © Sharon Cameron 2009

All rights reserved. No part of this book may be used or reproduced by any means, graphic, electronic, or mechanical, including photocopying, recording, taping or by any information storage retrieval system without the written permission of the publisher except in the case of brief quotations embodied in critical articles and reviews.

iUniverse books may be ordered through booksellers or by contacting:

iUniverse
1663 Liberty Drive
Bloomington, IN 47403
www.iuniverse.com
1-800-Authors (1-800-288-4677)

Because of the dynamic nature of the Internet, any Web addresses or links contained in this book may have changed since publication and may no longer be valid. The views expressed in this work are solely those of the author and do not necessarily reflect the views of the publisher, and the publisher hereby disclaims any responsibility for them.

ISBN: 978-1-4401-3395-4(pbk)
ISBN: 978-1-4401-3394-7(ebk)

Printed in the United States of America
iUniverse rev. date: 10/12/2009

To my friend Stacy,

who taught me the true meaning of friendship,

and without her intervention,

may never have given recovery a chance.

Some of the names in this book have been changed
to protect the privacy of the individuals.

Material in this book is for mature readers,
and may be triggering for individuals
struggling in early stages of recovery.
Reader discretion is advised.

All Scripture is taken from The Holy Bible,
New International Version unless otherwise noted.

Acknowledgments

So many people have touched my life, including many before my eating disorder began, and those I have gotten to know in the recent past. Those of you who know me well know my definition of a friend, and I thank you for being that to me (more than just jumping on the bandwagon and claiming to know me on Facebook).

To my wonderful family: Mom and Dad, thank you for your amazing love that only amazing parents like you can provide. Thank you for supporting me when times were tough. I love you....I couldn't ask for anything more from you.

Kristin, Curtis, Karen, Ramazan, Josh, and Amy... thank you for the ongoing support, prayers, talks, laughs, and for believing in me throughout my recovery and giving me encouragement along the way. I love you all so much!

And to my awesome nieces and nephew, Alayna, Zeke, and Eden—for the joy you all bring to me everytime

I see you, for the hugs, and for always making me laugh when I've needed it the most. ☺

To Victoria, for being the best counselor I could ever ask or hope for. I know you think I give you too much credit, but no one walked beside me as faithfully and as initmately as you did during my dark times. Thank you for putting up with my goofiness and many relapses, for your support and guidance, inspiring my creativity, never giving up on me, and continually directing me back to the love of Christ. One day we will work together and be friends in real life…I know it!

Katelyn, you don't understand how thankful I am that you are in my life! ☺ We are by far the most ridiculous people I know. I love that we could always find hilariousness (is that a word? I don't care! It's my book!) during our depression in early recovery, and still do every time we are together. You share my way of thinking and put up with my constant phone calls, rambling voice mails, and texts about my drama and random deep thoughts. Thank you for appreciating my stupid stories and laughing nonstop with me. The three greatest things are faith, hope, and love, and the greatest of these….is friendship.

Lane, fourteen years of best friendship and still going strong! No one else shares the bond that we have. I respect you so much as a person…thank you so much for always providing a listening ear even when you didn't completely understand. You are amazing, so much fun, and I know you will always be there, rain or shine. Yeah, I just love you, period (not Tom).

Nicole, thank you for being a great roommate to me these past three years! You dealt with a lot from me at times. Thank you for understanding, especially the night with unexpected paramedics breaking into our apartment. ☺ I'm so glad we get along well and can always talk and laugh together. I hope we will tell the story of moving twice within two weeks for years to come.

To Julie Norman, thank you for your passion to help those with eating disorders, and for being so down-to-earth and real. Thank you for the guidance you provided for me when I began recovery.

To my psychiatrist, Dr. Zaraa, thank you taking me as a patient when no one else would, and for providing the best treatment for me.

Monica, even though you didn't know me during my intense battle, you have provided so much love and encouragement to me, and have helped me choose to live many times. Your heart is so compassionate and genuine. Thank you for reminding me to be true to myself, and for being a beautiful example of a broken, reborn, and persevering woman. FYI...I'm so glad you get me...we are so similar it's scary!

And lastly, I thank God for showing me his perfect love and mercy again and again...only by his strength have I been able to find recovery and hope.

Foreward

When Sharon asked me to write the foreword for her book, I was deeply touched. Over the last several years I have watched the Lord call her out of the depths of addiction and into her journey with recovery. When Sharon first came to counseling in 2006, she was deeply in denial and a master at hiding the severity of her disorder. I witness this often with individuals who are just beginning the first stages of recovery from their addictions. They desire to get better...to be set free...yet are unwilling to say goodbye to their trusted companions...their best friend...their eating disorder.

In graduate school I learned the fundamental principles of treating clients with addictions. However, over the course of my early years in practice, I counseled very few individuals with eating disorders. It was not only foreign to my personal way of thinking, I was also a novice at treating this issue. Sharon inspired me to learn more about eating disorders, as well as seek new and innovative ways of treating those in bondage to this way of existing.

It was Sharon that introduced me to Remuda Ranch, and it was there that I found a well-rounded treatment program that addressed the whole person. I toured their facility and took training classes that allowed me to marry my own clinical foundation with a treatment approach to EDs (eating disorders) that offered success for those ready to embrace recovery. Remuda Ranch taught me that all eating disorders (or addictions for that matter) serve a purpose. The individual is trying in the best way they know how to get a healthy need met in an extremely unhealthy manner. They also recognize the significance of bringing Christ into the healing process. Without him, we are merely placing worldly band-aids on our deepest spiritual wounds.

Since this time, I have walked alongside clients and their families as they struggle with the power that the ED has over them. I have referred individuals to treatment centers when more intensive programming was needed. I have watched families grabble with our flawed health care system, when it fails to support the need for inpatient treatment because they were not close enough to death to justify this expense. I have witnessed firsthand the miracle of Christ's healing mercy when the client chose recovery over purging…starvation…their evil best friend.

When Sharon walked into my office all those years ago I would not have imagined that I would be learning from her as much as she was from me. I can see that she has a gift to minister to those that share her struggle with EDs. "To whom much is given, much is required" (Luke

12:48). Her gifts of art, writing, and creative expressions of feelings will bear much fruit for the Kingdom of God.

Whether you are struggling individually or love someone who is, her book will provide insight into the mind of an eating disordered person. Sharon is brave to open herself to this...she no longer is in denial or a master at hiding in the dark.

May God's peace, love, and light shine into your own life!

Victoria A. Gutbrod, MA. PCC-S

Introduction

When I began journaling about my struggle with an eating disorder over five years ago, I never dreamed it would evolve into a book of my journey through this tumultuous time in my life. I am writing this book as a recovering anorexic and bulimic. No, I'm not fully recovered, and I'm not going to say that I am. But I have no doubt in my mind that one day, I will be. So I have no shame in exposing my life, my thoughts, my lies, my hopes, and my dreams. I believe that if you are human, and you are holding this book in your hand, you will be able to relate in some way. Maybe not exactly to my struggles, but to the frustration of striving for perfection in a world that places worth on being the best, the strongest, the prettiest, or the smartest. I find it ironic that God desires the same from us. He has called each of us to holiness. But the beautiful part is that he knows we can't be. It isn't until we stop trying on our own to reach an unattainable goal, that we will experience God's power

As I grew up, I always had an older sibling as my idol. Maybe being the youngest in a big family made me feel lost. From a young age, I always wanted to be someone else. I never had contact with my oldest sister but I had more Amish siblings to churn butter with. I was close to Kristin, who is twelve years older than me, and wanted to be exactly like her. She was probably the most mature daughter, having to grow up quickly from the trauma my parents' oldest put on the family. Kristin set a path for me to follow in her footsteps, working two jobs in the summer, completing college in four years, and living at home before setting off securely in her career.

Karen and I hung out a lot when she was home from college and did goofy things together. I learned a little more about the real world from her experiences away from home. Eager to learn, I would ask countless questions. I was informed if you lived on a college campus, no one checked to make sure you went to class, or to church Sunday morning. I learned that going bowling at midnight involved loud music, flashing lights, and you could even glow in the dark if you wore white. This was fascinating. She also taught me how to listen to the radio quietly at night, so that I could actually be up on all the latest songs by the Spice Girls and N'Sync.

Josh and I became close, and since we were only five years apart, spent a lot of time together. Josh was the best older brother I could ever have. He included me in the baseball games with his friends, and let me hang out with them even though I'm sure most twelve-year-olds wouldn't want their little sister around. I became kind of a tomboy for a time in my childhood, and enjoyed playing football, baseball, and basketball with my big brother.

The best part about Josh is his sense of humor, and the fun we continue to share in our adult lives today.

I was observant, and paid attention to what my older siblings got praise for, and punished for. Getting a good grade in school was a fabulous achievement. Having a shady friend was not. Missing church was frowned upon. Helping with the dishes got compliments. Lying—out of the question. Staying out past curfew…well, that got my sister locked out, and I had to rescue her when she threw rocks at my window. That night she was dumped by a boyfriend, so I stayed up late to comfort her. I was a great twelve-year-old sis. Through these situations I learned how they dealt with things, how they answered questions asked by Mom and Dad, and definitely learned from their mistakes that got them into trouble. I wanted to be sure to avoid those at all costs.

I always was unhappy with who I was. I was discontent as Sharon, and wished, literally everyday, to be someone else. I tried constantly to imitate and ultimately be who my older siblings were, in order to be happy and approved of. Today I can see that it wasn't that I hated myself then, it was just that my own person did not exist. It was not *knowing* my identity that made me unhappy with who I was. I was pushing myself away, lost in comparisons with everyone around me, and had no idea who I was.

While I was young, I remember feeling the need to exercise every day. When I was as young as six or seven, I would make myself do one hundred crunches every day. I was always known as "little" and thin, and I would be sure to maintain that. One day I discovered Slim Fast in the cupboard, which was probably my mom's, and it looked good so I asked her what it was. She explained it was to drink if you wanted to lose weight, but I would never have to worry about that. I thought there could be nothing better than drinking chocolate milkshakes to lose weight, and so I tucked that idea in the back of my mind as a back up, in case one day I needed it. I was extremely active as a kid, always wanting to be involved in a sport of some kind. I played softball from the time I was five until I was twelve. Since I was so active, I rarely worried about my weight but I was sure to do crunches and pushups as often as I could.

I also began to do gymnastics at age nine. I learned cartwheels and handstands at a younger age, and in grade school began doing more advanced things on the playground. I had a friend who was competitive in gymnastics and would teach me new things. I finally talked my parents into letting me take lessons once a week, then later two days. I practiced constantly, at home, at school, and at the precious two hours a week I spent at gymnastics.

In junior high, I faced a lot of difficulties for the first time in my life. I was attending a new school, which I had chosen to go to. I lived closer to this district, and was able to attend by open enrollment. It was also a smaller school, which Josh had attended throughout high school. So, I decided to do what he did, because I wanted to be like him. I wrote out pros and cons lists about changing schools, and asked people for advice. I actually had decent decision-making skills at a young age, I simply did not really use them. Most of my decisions were not what I really wanted for myself; I did them to please someone else, or to be like someone else. I was new in seventh grade, and did not talk a whole lot. I made some friends, but experienced rejection and backstabbing from normal gossipy teenage girls. I hated school, and felt alone and afraid of ever going back the next year. Luckily, being so involved in my church youth group, I made three close friends, two of which are still good friends today. I also convinced my parents to let me try out a new gym, a YMCA, which had a competitive gymnastics team. I took lessons throughout my seventh grade year, and was invited to be on the level five team the next. My parents made huge commitments and sacrifices to pay for the lessons and drive me three days a week to the gym. I was very thankful, because it was the only place I felt safe and accepted by everyone. I met my best friend Lane that year, and we have stuck together ever since we were twelve. The gym was the only place I wanted to be, and I loved every minute of it. Some of my favorite memories today are from the sweaty, goofy, sometimes grueling days at gymnastics practice and meets.

At church, I began to meet one-on-one with a woman involved with the youth group. I felt that I needed to do so in order to be a good Christian. I learned so much in these years, and grew in my faith. The only problem was the intense push to be perfect, which was only emphasized in our weekly meetings. I remember her telling me that she would go a year or so without ever missing a day reading the Bible and in prayer. I assumed I had to live up to this standard, and that if I failed, I was not acceptable in God's eyes.

In high school, I finally started to open up to my friends at school. I wasn't popular, but wasn't a total loser either. My freshman year went well for the most part, and I continued to strive for perfect grades to please my parents and myself. As the perfect daughter and student, I began to notice that my parents praised me when I did really well, but if I did make a mistake, which of course I inevitably did, they seemed to focus on that. If I got all A's and one A-, it seemed like the A- was the focus. I know they did not intentionally do this, and sometimes it was only jokingly, but it reinforced my desire for perfection, and I connected that with love and acceptance.

At church, I began to experience unbelievable pain from people who I thought were supposed to be loving Christians. I felt judged and never good enough. Several incidents of confronting minor situations, or personal matters, such as being late to church, or missing an event began to make me feel like a horrible, sinful person. The more they happened, the worse and worse I began to feel, and the less I began to value myself. I was receiving total opposite messages, that God was forgiving, loving and thought so much of me, yet I was told I was crap, couldn't do anything right, and was a failure for not being perfect.

I continued getting good grades in school, and having a blast in gymnastics. The YMCA was a positive experience for me. It wasn't the same as many gyms that encourage weight loss or focus on weight. We were encouraged to eat healthy and work hard to stay in shape, but no one ever told me or anyone else I know of, to lose weight. However, constantly being in a leotard and seeing my reflection in mirrors of my every move kept me aware of my weight. I did what I could to maintain a "perfect" body. I went to practice three times a week for two and a half hours, and did conditioning every day in addition to that. Sometimes I would run on my days off as well, for endurance. I would occasionally restrict, mostly at lunch because my mom was not around to see. If she did notice I was skipping a meal at home, she would harshly tell me I wasn't going to do that. The fact that I didn't start my period until I was almost sixteen probably scared her into thinking I wasn't eating enough, and she would warn me of osteoporosis if I didn't take care of my body. I probably wasn't eating as much as I should have during puberty, because of my intense fear of gaining weight, and the exercising I'm sure didn't help. But I didn't intentionally do anything to lose weight. When my mom tried to express her concern, I simply brushed it off and thought, "Oh well, it can't be that bad." My Amish parents and I were never close while I was growing up because my mom was busy quilting and my dad was working in the fields –I'm sorry—he actually was a teacher (but my mom really does quilt). My mom and I didn't talk like many girls do with their mom. I do regret this and think that if we could have had open communication we would have had a better relationship.

At the beginning of my junior year, I began to have a strong desire for freedom. I began to get angry with my dad for not allowing me to have the same freedom as my friends. I got my license but wasn't allowed to drive very much. He was just trying to watch out for his little girl, but I felt like a child and controlled. I was only allowed to drive during the day, and couldn't drive anywhere at night. I didn't understand the rules that I couldn't drive myself home from a friend's house at ten o'clock because it was dark out, but I could ride home with anybody at a later hour. In my mind, I was the perfect kid who never did anything wrong, and I felt that if my dad should trust anyone, it should be his own daughter. I know that he did, but he was just worried about letting me grow up. But this made me feel like I wasn't good enough and incapable of even doing normal things for my age, like driving a car. But I don't know if driving a horse and buggy would have been any different. I would have probably gotten run over by a Hummer.

This year was the beginning of my rebellion. I hated my life and hated not being in control of my own decisions. The more rules that were put on me, the more I found ways to sneak around them. This makes me laugh because I still never did anything terrible. I would stay out later with my friends then spend the night at someone's house so my parents didn't know, or go t.p.ing at 2 a.m., or watch movies I was never allowed to watch at home— anything I could think of that I wouldn't get in too much trouble for, but was against my parents' strict rules. Even though I felt good for doing things I wasn't supposed to, I did feel guilty for the lies I constantly told to answer the questions my parents asked. Sometimes I wanted to tell them that I did things they didn't approve of, just to let them know I wasn't as perfect as they thought, but I was too scared to give up that identity. I think in a way I was so used to trying to be perfect, but so sick of it at the same time. Although we weren't close, my mom and I didn't really fight either. I'm glad that I did not argue with her during my teenage years, because I didn't get along well with my dad, and felt awful and guilty because of it. I figured even if I didn't get along with him, at least it was better than fighting with both of them.

I began to be depressed this year, when I was sixteen. I didn't ever want to admit I was, because I was told depressed people were just "in sin," and I didn't even think I was depressed at the time. I had quit gymnastics that summer for a couple of weeks, because I felt that I wanted to do other things, and found myself even more alone and unsure of who I was without that. I went back and decided to compete again that year, but my body was changing and it was hard to get back in shape. This was the first time in my life I noticed I gained weight, and I hated myself for it. But I stuck to gymnastics and tried my best to work out as much as I could.

That spring, I decided to attend post secondary for half a day my senior year. I barely got to make this decision for myself, because my dad told me I wasn't allowed to. Here I was, seventeen years old, an age most people are gaining more independence and moving on with their lives, while my parents were telling me not to. His explanation was that he was worried about me being there and driving there, and so I couldn't go. My reasoning was that Josh had done it, and I was a responsible and smart girl who wouldn't do anything stupid, and who wanted to face the world and be challenged by college. Almost every answer to that was that, "Well, Josh is a boy, it's different." I didn't understand why he got a car when he was sixteen had a ton of freedom in regards to driving and to his curfew, and was able to attend parties and go dancing in high school. I never even really attempted to go to parties because I was too embarrassed to ask for a ride or leave early when everyone else could drive themselves. Anyways, I finally convinced my dad to allow me to go to college for a couple classes, and he at first was hesitant to let me drive. Luckily, he finally loosened up and let me drive myself mostly, occasionally carpooling with two other girls. I was accepted at the University of Akron and excited to be out in a new Amish-free world, complete with electricity and alcohol (once again…kidding) and hopefully gain more independence by proving I could handle it.

One Sunday morning after a sleepover, my two best friends and I got up and stopped for a cup of coffee on the way to church and walked in five minutes late to the worship in the youth group. The youth pastor made sure to include in the sermon about how some of us didn't make Sunday morning a priority, and church was the one place you should never be late. I began to get intense anger when such statements were made, because I knew my heart was in the right place. I wanted to be at church, and didn't think it mattered to God if I was a couple of minutes late, because that was better than going with a bad attitude and being an hour early. I still don't understand the fact that a bunch of teenagers, who need encouragement, love, and support were told they were not good enough and torn apart so frequently. I hated that and I knew it wasn't right, but I kept going along with it because I was afraid to tell them how I felt, and I thought maybe eventually I could earn their approval.

One of the biggest influences on me in my high school years was the need to live up to other Christian's standards. I was never taught to make decisions based on my own convictions. The church taught that Christianity was "black and white," either you were godly, or you weren't. You did exactly what they said, or you were wrong. So many assumptions were made, and confrontations that were simply prideful and wrong. One incident I remember vividly was when I did not want to go on a winter retreat that year, due to the fact that they were always so negative. A statement was made that anyone not going was in sin. I signed up for it that morning and forked over the fifty dollars that night.

Numerous times, I remember going to the leaders, usually with a friend, and trying to express my feelings. I told them that I had the exact same faith and love for God that they did, although to me, it didn't include the outward acts of being in *every* Bible study and *every* event, following *every* rule, and spending an hour or more a day in intense theological Bible study and prayer. *Numerous* times we had these conversations, only leading me to tears of frustration for not being heard, and usually a lecture on submission to my elders. They were always right, everyone else was always wrong. I was trapped in my personal relationship with God, and at the same time, balancing my act of perfection, not even knowing if I was trying to please man, myself, or the Lord. But it was all I knew, and it was what I was always drawn back into.

I was excited for my senior year, and felt that maybe for once I would have some independence. I did, and was relieved of my depression for a short time. School went well, and while I wasn't the best one on the team, gymnastics was simply a lot of fun. I loved every minute I was there, and made lasting friendships and memories. I lost five or ten pounds by eating better and working out at the gym. I really didn't notice it, but sometimes people would comment. I liked the way I looked and honestly don't know how much I weighed then. I wasn't trying to control it, and I believe I ate in moderation. Being a competitive gymnast, I probably exercised more than the average person, but I still think it was at a healthier level than it would become later on in my disorder.

That spring I discovered I was rejected from Grove City College. I took it hard because I really wanted to go away to college, and I hated rejection because it was a realization I wasn't as good as everyone else who got accepted. I was given three choices for college, continuing at the University of Akron or Kent State University and commuting (I wasn't allowed to live on campus), or attending Grove City because it was a Christian college. Of course out of these options, I chose Grove City as my first choice, because I wanted and needed to get away from the control in my life by my parents. I didn't really even want to go there, I just actually wanted to get away from the whole Christian bubble world I was raised in. I would have never picked Grove City if it were completely up to me, but it was the only place that I felt I would be in control of my life. I ended up not even being the first person to read my letter of rejection, as my mom opened it and told me over the phone. I chose to go to Kent State, mostly because my dad wanted me to stay at Akron.

Graduation was amazing, and I graduated as salutatorian. This is one accomplishment I am proud of. I didn't put pressure on myself to be valedictorian, because I knew it wasn't possible for me. Josh had also been salutatorian, so I guess that gave me comfort in knowing I was at least equal to him. I thought that maybe if I were as good as my brother, my parents would accept me the same.

My summer went well for the most part at church.

I was slowly distancing myself from things leaders would say. When the pastor lectured all the girls and told us we weren't godly, I got mad but I didn't believe it. Even when we were condemned for watching *Legally Blonde*, my friends and I stuck to watching awesome chick flicks such as *How to Lose a Guy in 10 Days, The Wedding Planner,* and *Coyote Ugly* (gasp!). During a vacation Bible school, the leaders told the girls we were a stumbling block to the guys in one-piece bathing suits, so I whipped out my attitude and put on jeans and a hoodie while dragging kids down the slip and slide, lest one of the guys would lust over my sexiness. I could see the absurdity, but since I was insanely caught up in legalism, I still felt like I had to follow their rules for approval.

I was still exercising every day, and vowed to myself to run four miles every day that summer. I didn't think it was too much to aim for. I told my sister-in-law, Amy, that I was going to run every morning no matter what and she said, "Don't you think that's a lot of exercise?" I quickly denied it and told her that I enjoyed it and did not feel in bondage to it. I didn't quite meet my goal, but I tried, and felt that I had to replace gymnastics with a crazy amount of running.

In August, my two friends Lane and Nicole moved away to attend college in Cincinnati, Ohio. I was alone, and disappointed in myself, knowing that I could have had what they did, if I had been good enough or just performed a little better. While I definitely had more freedom at home now that I was in college, I still had a curfew, and hated living at home. I hated church because I was constantly ripped apart while I was there and I hated adjusting to college because it was hard to make friends

CHAPTER 3

Something finally convinced my dad that it would be okay for me to apply at a restaurant near my house. It was owned by Christians and my dad was probably comforted in that fact, even though I know he was still worried about me getting harassed by customers, and not being about to take the stress. Ironically, two years later, I reported a manager for sexual harassment, not only to me, but to many of the younger women on the staff. I was hired there and so glad to have a job where I would actually be making money and doing something most college students did. Having a change in job, and the summer ahead made me a little bit happier. I decided to train for a marathon, which was that October (2004). I did it for enjoyment, and didn't even really stick to my training schedule like I should have. Most people told me that three months wasn't long enough to train, but I was set on proving them wrong. I trained for the half-marathon, and was prepared to run that. But when I approached mile thirteen, I thought, "I can keep going," and I told myself that every mile after it. I finished all 26.2 miles in just under five hours. I still can't really believe I did that, as I had never run farther than ten miles in my life, and was purging quite a bit earlier that week. I am so blessed not to have messed up my body due to my unhealthy behaviors. I can seriously laugh about it now, when I think about the fact that I couldn't walk for two days after, as my legs were so sore. However, I thrived on the pain, feeling pride in the pain that proved I had worked hard to achieve what I wanted.

I was proud of finishing the marathon but after I began worrying that I would get out of control with eating and my weight if I didn't continue running. I took about a week off, but went back to overexercising and purging. Throughout the winter, my depression became worse again, and I began to admit my problem to some other close friends. They listened, but didn't really understand my struggle, and didn't know what to say. They suggested I get help, but I still didn't think it was that bad of a problem, and I was afraid to admit to my mom that I was still doing it. Slowly, it became normal to throw up what I ate, and eat just to throw it up. I planned how long I would starve, when I would binge, when and where I would purge, and when I could exercise. If I wasn't obsessing about this, I was doing schoolwork, or working. I tried to have relationships but I couldn't, because I didn't let myself get close to anyone, and I never wanted to go out or do anything with friends because it would probably involve food.

*   *   *   *

June 20, 2004
Dear Father,

I love you. I have such a wonderful family, so many friends, a great job, a church I am learning to like, and most of all, I have you. God, forgive me for my sin this past week. I don't want to yield to sin, especially not going back to how I was living in the past. Help me to keep my eyes looking forward, and to continue striving and pressing on. I want you more and more each day. And any day without this desire is wasted. Only what I do for you, Lord is worthwhile. Only your work will last.

I am so grateful for the sermon today, and helping me realize I will be tempted, but how I deal with it is so much more important. It is not right to feed desires just so they'll go away. They will only come back stronger. I'm sorry for thinking I was standing firm, then choosing sin over obedience. Please continue to transform me into an image of you, beautiful and holy. Amen.

July 18, 2004
Lord,

I want to fall at your feet. I confess my laziness, my lack of prayer in pursuing you lately. I don't know why, but tiredness or busyness has taken priority over you. Why is my life so monotonous? It shouldn't be. I'm so busy sometimes I do nothing. I'm caught in a rush...then have nothing accomplished at the end of the day. What is accomplished? I don't know if I ever accomplish anything. I don't want to live to accomplish exercise everyday anymore, or for what I'm going to eat or not eat. It frustrates me that I'm still struggling but I know I'm making progress. Whenever I want to turn back please remind me of the horror and that I want to be happy like I am now.

I want to learn from my mistakes and try not to have very many regrets. God—I WANT TO LIVE FOR YOU! I really do…that's what it comes down to. Please radically change me, make me a more passionate Christian. You found me, you rescued me, you saved me, and you deserve all of me, my life, all that I can do, all you can do through me. I'm confused, but I know you're not. Amen.

August 29, 2004
God,

I felt so out of control today. I wanted so badly to stop myself but I didn't. God, I don't know what to do. I am sorry! I really am. I don't want to live my life this way. All I can do is humble myself before you and ask you to please forgive me. I don't understand your love; I've failed you so much. Why do I keep falling?!? It's almost been a year since the first time. A YEAR. A year of my life I've wasted and brought pain to myself by making myself throw up. I'm sorry. I don't know what to do. I think I'm happy, then all of a sudden, I'm not. Please radically help me. Change my heart and my life. Please let tomorrow be a new day, a day I don't think about my body or food. Help me to know when I need to eat and how much. Please help me to trust you. I feel like I need more of you in whatever form. Please bless this semester. Amen.

September 20, 2004
Dear God,

There's so much on my mind right now. I have to pour

Last Sunday I felt so weird after I threw up. It made my body hurt and I had a headache and felt like I was going to pass out. My muscles were sore and all I wanted to do was relax and get better. I drank Gatorade and that helped. I know it dehydrates your body but I don't know why I felt so weird. Anyways, I don't know who to talk to or what to do so I think I will try not to throw up and lose a little bit of weight. I've done it before, so I can do it again. All I need is one good day of eating well and then I can get going. I need to put my plan in writing so I can actually stick to it:

Don't eat anything in the morning.

Eat a small lunch.

Nothing until dinner. No snacks before or after.

NO junk food!!!!

Drink only water!

Exercise everyday.

That should do it. I will do it or this crazy cycle will go on and on and on. I can't do that.

October 17, 2004

My day didn't go too bad. I still feel like I ate too much even when I probably didn't. I could have gone without the Pop Tarts. Other than that, I had a sandwich, yogurt, pear, soup, and carrots. Not too bad. I still have tomorrow and I'll exercise soon for a while. I think I'll feel better after that. When I think about it, depriving myself of some food isn't that bad when I remember the results I can achieve… thinness. To me it's worth it.

October 19, 2004

I've been doing so well with not eating too much and

throwing up. Yesterday all I ate was soup, yogurt, a little lasagna, a breadstick, and salad. Not bad...I actually felt in control. Today, I did okay too—good, even. I haven't eaten anything yet. I don't want to get to the point where I'm like really sick. I just want to lose 10-15 pounds. I really feel like it's possible this time.

October 25, 2004

Today at church we were asked what we hunger for. I guess when I think about it, I hunger for a lot of worldly things. I crave success, and outward accomplishments, and to be noticed. That goes along with the eating and body issues. I feel that if I look a certain way or weigh less I will have one up on someone else who may not. But I think it's also just me. I have high standards for myself and am not happy if I fail. I also hunger for love. I want to be loved by one guy and to love him back. I feel empty in that area of my relationships because I don't have that.

October 26, 2004
Dear God,

I want to pray right now as your child whom you love even though it is hard for me to believe right now. I haven't taken the time to pray to you in a long time. And I know there's no point in "getting right" with you without taking it seriously and it's not a one time thing. It is a process and I hope I can eventually. Being honest with myself, I realize I have a problem. If I'm not throwing up, I'm starving. And if I'm eating, I'm throwing up or wishing I could. Yesterday surprised me. I threw up the first chance I got. I hate it but I continue. Please make me hate it more. Then today it feels so good not to eat, like I'm making up for yesterday and what I did. I was also lonely and depressed. Now, the control is still there, but it's for different reasons. I pretty much have freedom now and make my own decisions. I am prideful and want to be better and better than everyone. It's more of a perfection thing, too. Because I diet so much and when I do eat it feels like I've failed and I have to throw up or my day will be ruined. I think I'm afraid of failure. I hate failing. I want every aspect of my life to be perfect or to be the best. I have to get straight A's or I'll be a failure. I have to have friends and have a guy like me or I'm a failure. I have to run for an hour or more everyday or I'll be a failure. I have to eat healthy or I fail. And I have to lose weight or I'm a failure. It's an obsession.

The strange thing is, I don't feel bad, or sad about it. I'm actually very happy and satisfied. Continually striving for more, but happy with the progress. I think I have lost about five pounds—which doesn't sound like a lot but that's five less than before and can soon turn into ten. I'm getting there.

So, Kelly and I also talked about God and how we don't really have a desire to live that way. I honestly don't see the point of living a lie. Why be fake and cover up what I'm truly feeling and thinking? I hate the person I used to be and I refuse to continue being it. I still love God, but right now I'm doing fine and I don't want to change. It's partly the effort it would take. I don't want to. I've tried and I need help but there isn't anyone to help me. Someday I will find the answers but it will be awhile, and I have to be ready. Kelly wasn't trying to make me change. She was just saying how it is probably better to try to stop now than if it continues to get worse—which I do agree with. She doesn't say, "just eat" or stupid things like that. No one can make me eat.

December 8, 2004

Wow, so many things as usual. Yesterday was good, I think it was a turning point, but in a bad way. Kelly and I hung out and talked about it some more, and she told me I looked thinner and looked good. Then she thought she shouldn't have said that, that it might encourage me negatively, which it did but I'm not telling her that. When she said that, something clicked because I thought I had lost weight but she was the only one to notice or say anything. Then I got home and couldn't run because it was too late but I worked out in my room forever. Then, today, I have no desire to eat because I know what I have been doing has been working. I just have to keep trying. It seems more achievable now, and I won't quit until I get what I want.

I feel bad talking to people about it now though, because they want to help, but I don't really want it and I feel like the conversation never goes anywhere. It does help to talk to someone who will listen. I guess I am just waiting for one of two things to happen:

1. Magically get better—it will just all go away.

2. Lose the weight I want, stay there, and be okay.

I hope I can recover and not feel the need to throw up after I eat and not be afraid to eat. Not eating very much is the only solution I can think of because then I don't want to throw up.

It's also weird being referred to by Kelly as "her friend with an eating disorder." I guess I have one but I can't really say it. It's weird that she is the one who wants to help me after I told other people last year and I actually wanted help but no one would. Now I don't really want to get better. I just think it's so weird she brought it up, because everyone else either assumes I'm okay or is afraid to ask.

January 13, 2005
    Yogurt, orange, sandwich, water
    Today, my health goals are to drink only water and just eat one meal. So I'm doing well but it's only 2:40. I'm not going to eat anything at work. I'm going to keep making goals for each day for what I'll eat. Then, I'll know if I succeeded. Tomorrow I will allow myself one drink besides water and one meal—no junk food at all.

January 14, 2005
12:00 a.m.
    So, I failed. That's why I set goals—so I know when I fail. I was so depressed at work. I couldn't even talk to anyone or smile. I want to be so much skinnier and have people notice. I ate normally for about 2 weeks, and then started to throw up on Sunday because I was home alone for quite a while. It makes me feel terrible, like I'll never be happy again, and like I have the most out of control life of anyone I know. So, I have good days and I have bad days. Monday was an awesome day! I just don't think I can be happy until I lose weight. When I lose weight, I'm happy. I like impressing people; I like when they notice.

January 30, 2005
God,
    I've neglected you too long! I love you. I miss you! Forgive

me for my foolishness. I need you to lift me up and hold me. Take away my desires to throw up. Even as I am week and struggle, be by my side and lead me on, in your grace. I would be so lost without you. I thank you for accepting me as your own. I don't deserve it at all. I'm so sorry I didn't care about you for so long. Thank you for renewing my joy. I so need you alone and I want you to restore our relationship. Give me the strength to fix the areas I've done wrong. Please, help me! I'm tired of thinking about food all the time and worrying about my body. It won't make me happy! I'll never be satisfied. You have shown me that. Continue to guide me to leave this area of sin in my life. Amen.

February 1, 2005
God,

Ahh!!!!! I am so frustrated with my decisions, body, eating, starving, etc. I wish I could cry; I really do, but I don't feel like I can. I want to talk to someone but the right person never seems available. I know you are though! You draw me close and hold me near when I need you most.

Sunday, I ate and threw up and Monday I didn't even eat much all day. Then, I had yogurt and I threw it up! I can't really believe I actually did. It was yogurt! I don't know why, even, I wanted to get it out of my body. I feel sick when I eat, a lot of the time, probably from throwing up so much. I feel like I can't get anywhere on my own. My ideas always end up in failure. Please send help. Whether it is a book or person or whatever. I really do trust your amazing and awesome power. Amen.

what was left to my parents' house, so they wouldn't go to waste—not like I had never wasted food before. As I purged alone in the empty house, I felt disgusted. I had wasted two hours of my day and accomplished nothing. I didn't want to do anything, except lie on the floor and wish that what happened this day would never happen again.

Unfortunately, it did. It happened too many days to even count. And the times that were not this extreme, I would still throw up on days I thought I ate too much and found myself alone. I decided to stay home and be productive one Friday night. Stacy and her boyfriend had asked me to go to a haunted house with them but I forced myself to go work out after work. When I was home, I sat at my computer, but wanted to do nothing but eat. This compelled me to go buy food, eat, and throw up. I cried and cried after, wishing I hadn't let it happen. I sat back down to do some homework but the inner voice drove me to the bathroom to continue vomiting. I couldn't stop. When Stacy got home, she asked me, "So what did you do tonight? Homework?" My books were still lying in front of my, open yet unread. My computer screen was blank before me. This was the first time I realized my eating disorder controlled me. And I was scared.

*   *   *   *

June 8, 2005
Dear God,

I am only happy when I'm near to you! I can't be happy or find happiness unless I'm with you, close to you. I had so much time yesterday to think while I was at work because it was so slow. It is both good and bad. Good because I realize things, bad because I start to worry. The more I think, the more things come up that I worry about. You have everything in control! I don't need to worry! But there are so many thoughts I have and I can't even describe my feelings. I am happy with my life. I'm happier even now, talking to you. I don't know what to read, but I want to read my Bible! Please guide me to the right passage. Encourage me, as you do so often. I want to write too. Please give me ideas and words and tell me how I can best verbalize my feelings and thoughts. God—you gave me this life. It's sad sometimes to think of how fleeting it is, but it is meant to be enjoyed! Help me to live with enjoyment, with love, with purpose. I need you to be happy. Doing a bunch of things doesn't make me happy, even if it is with friends. I felt like such a failure yesterday. Giving my battle with food over to you is exactly that—a daily struggle. But you will help, I know you will. And you will teach me so much and bring me into closer fellowship with you and I will be more in love with you. The struggle won't be over until we're in Heaven. And then I will struggle no more. It will be wonderful. But the temporary pain and hard times and battle with sin on this earth are worth it—worth it because of you, because of Christ. You give me hope. Thank you for your forgiveness and love. Thank you for hope and blessings. God—you will do amazing things, I know it! Please make me in awe, even as things are hard. Life is hard; each day is a battle. But it is a choice—a commitment for you, I can ignore, or I can embrace. I want to embrace you today—embrace you completely. A bunch of things won't make me happy today. I need to be with you. Amen.

needs is you. May you be enough to solve her problems. Use me in whatever way you can. I am so thankful you placed us to be together at this time. I appreciate her friendship so much. I really do. It is so nice just to have a friend to hang out with and talk with, rather than living by myself or with my parents. And I know you wanted her to be with someone who can understand what she's going through. Even though my struggle is in a different way, I can relate. I know what it's like to be sucked in and controlled by food and it's scary to watch it happen to a close friend. Please save her—rescue her from it now! Do something amazing!!!

CHAPTER 5

My eating disordered behaviors worsened through the summer of '05, and I began compulsively exercising which carried on through my junior year of college. In the fall, I began a quest for help again, knowing that what I was doing wasn't good, and I knew I was stuck in this cycle. I wanted someone to listen, understand my problem, and tell me what to do. Stacy began to be more concerned, because she would hear me throwing up at night, and she would never see me eat. Out of shame and desperate for help from someone, I asked her what to do. She suggested talking to a lady at work, who worked with college students at her church. I decided to give it a try.

I was currently exercising every day, driving twenty-five minutes just to go to the rec center at Kent to workout. I would go to class from 9 a.m. to 7 p.m. every Tuesday and Thursday, ending with a two hour workout, and spend my days off working, doing homework, and driving back to Kent to exercise too. I don't ever remember missing a day. I would even go on the weekends after work on Friday and Saturday night, not caring how much of a loser I was for not having a life. I was really proud of myself to have such discipline while everyone else blew off exercise for the weekend. I was able to drop some weight, but nothing too drastic yet.

I met with the woman from work for coffee one day, and tried to explain my problem. She talked most of the time, and I didn't feel that she was understanding or a very good listener. She told me she recommended I tell my family, and gave me a book to read. I didn't feel that either of those things would help me, so I rejected her. I pushed her away and told her after that that I decided I didn't want her help, I was happy with living this way, and sorry to bother her.

One thing that she said that triggered me in this conversation was, "You're not that bad yet, and you can still go to work and school." I took that as a slap in the face. I thought that she was crazy, telling me that not eating, binging and purging (now up to four or five times a day), and doing nothing in my free time except exercise was a pretty big problem. I also figured that I was thinner than in the past but obviously not thin enough to even look like I had a problem. This pushed me in the negative direction, only to be sure to make my eating disorder worse in order for people to notice and care.

I began restricting more, eating very rigid and few times a day. For about two months, I lived on Slim Fast bars, eating three a day. The only exception was episodes of binging and purging, or a small meal I would allow myself once a week. This allowed me to be somewhat social, and eat something so no one would notice I was starving myself. I was depressed and simply went through my days, isolated in the busyness of life. School, work, working out, and my eating disorder monopolized my time. I continued this routine throughout the semester, and managed to get a 4.0, even though I probably spent more time at the rec than at class. I had to do everything perfectly, and even though my relationships were falling apart, I couldn't really see it then.

*   *   *   *

August 31, 2005
Dear God,

  What if all I've ever felt, ever said, and ever prayed was just a lie? What if everything I've ever done was just a show, and I didn't mean it, and I didn't believe it? I don't want that to be the case, but I don't know sometimes if I'm for real. I know you are. I don't know how or why, I just believe. My fear is that I am a liar, an insincere person, or I don't know, maybe just tricked myself into believing I'm something I'm not. Please don't let that be true! I know something is missing when I'm apart from you. I am not complete. I'm not happy. But when I'm close to you—or what I believe is close to you—I am so joyful and satisfied.

  I feel life is so pointless sometimes. All people try to do is make the most money or get as successful as they can, then they die and lose it all. Or even school—it's pointless. You learn and learn and obtain as much knowledge as you can, for what? To be smart, get a job, and make money, then you die. No one cares that you were smart, unless you write it

Thursday goes well. I'm talking to Rachel. I'm scared I won't be able to say what I feel. I want to tell her the truth though. I'm afraid I really don't care all that much about "getting better" and it all a waste of time. I don't know. I just hope it goes well.

I think I want help. I believe that I do sometimes. I want the pain to go away. I want to eat and not throw up and to not even want to throw up. I want to not be afraid of eating or of food. But I have an unwavering drive to lose weight, stay thin, control food, etc., etc. And just when I think I'm on track to getting better, I seem to take 100 steps back. And it's worse than before and I'm unhappier and find myself in a terrible mess. I really don't know what I want anymore. People like Stacy don't know what it is that I truly want and need. I don't want to be "on a diet" the rest of my life. She said, "Just eat salads if you have to, it's boring but if that's what you have to do." All I do eat is salads and Slim Fast bars lately. It doesn't work. Plus that's not the point of true recovery. I want to have a freedom with food like people who I know used to struggle with eating disorders and now can eat any food and not have any restrictions. I can't even imagine allowing myself to eat anything and not have safe/ unsafe or good/bad foods. I seriously can't. But if I do decide to get better I am going to go all the way. I don't want to "sort of" recover and still obsess about food and exercise and diet the rest of my life. It will be 100% committed, or I'll just continue on in my rut, up and down. I don't know but I just really need to talk to someone who cares about me and shows me that they do.

November 14, 2005
All I ate today was a Slim Fast bar, salad, and fruit.

So, why do I feel so fat??? I even ran three miles, biked five, and ellipticalled three. I think I burned 700 calories, yet I still don't look or feel thin enough. Tomorrow is a three Slim Fast bar day, one for each meal for a total of 660 calories. Plus I'll go to the rec twice. I will go twice on Wednesday too and I will only eat a little. I might allow myself coffee at Borders or a snack because I've been so good lately. If that's all I eat all day, then it's okay. It's not the healthiest but who cares? All the working out will make up for it and keep me from throwing up.

I almost want to starve myself and look bad so Rachel and other people will visibly be able to tell something is wrong. Then maybe someone will want to help. I've been eating this way for two weeks. It is working. I have noticed I've lost a little bit, but no one else has really noticed yet. I'm holding off on weighing myself until someone asks if I've lost weight. They will...I just have to be patient and maybe lose a little more. I'm hungry now. It's only 8:30 p.m. That's good. I'm happy.

November 17, 2005

Yesterday, I ran four miles, ellipticalled four miles, biked one and a half miles for a total of 500 + 400 + 50 calories. 950. ☺ That made up for what I ate, even though it wasn't all that much—a pretzel, fruit, and chocolate covered pretzels. I don't even feel that hungry and I haven't even eaten since 5:00 p.m. (it's 8:00 a.m.). I do have a Slim Fast bar I'll eat later. Eating like this keeps me from binging/purging. I love being hungry and I love my body now that I'm losing weight.

gain a pound I'll just lose it. And more. I can't get help now. I don't feel bad, I can't even cry. I wish I could sometimes. I think what I hate the most is my inability to open up to anyone. I seriously can't. I can't talk to someone and reveal how I really feel; I can't ever be completely honest. It might be because I'm afraid of what they'll think, or because I'm afraid I'll have to change, and what people will expect or that they'll look at me different and know I'm not "perfect." I don't want to give up that status. As miserable as this makes me, I feel that it empowers me, now that I finally am achieving the body I want. But I can't think right. I am illogical and don't use my brain. It drives me crazy because I'm a smart person. I know I am. But what I'm doing just is so far from smart. I can't even concentrate to write in here...I wish I could.

November 30, 2005

I am convinced that I don't have that bad of a problem. I feel like other people want to tell me I do...but I'm not anorexic because I don't think I've lost enough weight, and I'm not bulimic because I don't binge and purge twice a week. I think I'm okay. I probably don't have the healthiest eating habits, but that's okay. That's why I'm dieting in December. Seriously dieting. Slim Fast bars will be my meals most days—I have never been so determined to be skinny. Well, I am skinny now. I want to be skinnier though. At work, I'll just have salads or skip lunch when I can. Pretzels are safe to eat and also yogurt. I'm going to stop buying snacks and then I'll save money too. I can't gain back the 10 pounds I've lost. I wish I didn't push people away who try to get close to me. I don't know why. I guess I'm scared of rejection, of being ultimately hurt. I do a lot of things I despise, and things I wish that I didn't do.

I was thinking yesterday, where does motivation come from? Is it internal or external? What gives you the drive for something? I think it's internal. No one ever pushed me to lose weight. I guess models, the media, or other thin girls motivate me. But mostly I motivate myself, just by wanting it so bad and continuing being unsatisfied. My failures motivate me to do better.

I wish I could have someone to be 100% open and honest with. I will find someone. I hope I find someone. This isolation is driving me insane.

December 5, 2005

I think that losing weight makes me feel good. I know it does. But after a while of being at a new weight, I get used to it and then I don't feel that skinny anymore like I did at the beginning. I still do, I still am, yet I am used to it. A friend said, "You look skinny," to me at work on Saturday. These three words—"You look skinny"—made my day. I was worried I had gained weight back or something for a week or so. But I'm okay. ☺

Today I had a sourdough pretzel (100 calories) for breakfast, and then I'll have a salad for lunch, then nothing else. I'll try to just drink water at work. Then run of course, tonight. My goal is to lose 5 pounds by Friday.

December 6, 2005

I didn't write as much as I wanted to yesterday. I have too many thoughts going through my head right now to write them all down. I feel so unemotional. Happy is the only feeling I have, and anger. I can't be sad or scared or stressed. I was mad last night at Stacy and I didn't even feel bad for yelling at her. It was weird; I felt nothing. Ordinarily I would have cried or at least felt bad, but I couldn't. I tried. I wasn't sorry for what I said. It's true. She doesn't eat enough, obviously, or she wouldn't pass out. I'm sick of hearing her sob stories about all her problems ("I'm freezing, my butt hurts, my clothes don't fit, I passed out..."). No shit, Stacy. That's what happens when you weigh nothing and don't eat. You gain your weight you need to back, not pass out, get your period, and eat normally, and THEN you have my permission to yell at me! She doesn't eat! At least I'll admit it. I'm not the one denying the fact I don't eat completely right. I am starving myself. I haven't eaten a real meal in two weeks! And I do make myself throw up. I never said I didn't. I refuse to talk about it anymore. She just doesn't get it. She makes things worse. She brings it up. She should know it makes me upset when she points out how skinny people are, including herself. There's nothing I can say to help her because she needs to eat if she wants to gain weight and not pass out or whatever. I guess I'll just avoid her for a few days until I feel like I can talk to her without getting mad. Why in the world did I move in with her?!? What was I thinking?

I realized yesterday that I am also mad at Rachel. I'm mad at the fact that she didn't listen to me. She talked the whole time! Why can't anyone just listen to what Sharon is feeling!?! They all feel the need to jump in and first of all, jump to conclusions, and second, try to solve my problems. She just talked and shoved a book in my face and told me that's what would fix my life. Whatever. Sometimes I do want someone to help me fix my problems. But I want them to understand me first. Rachel probably couldn't even say what my problem is exactly if I asked her or if someone else asked. She just thinks I throw up. She probably thinks I eat but then also binge and purge. Well, she has no idea, and what I am doing is probably worse. She thinks I want to get better, while actually I write about my continued success at starving and keep striving to lose more weight.

Yesterday I ate good! Then today: one pretzel (100 calories) and two Slim Fast bars (440 calories)=540! I have to go to the dentist tomorrow. Hopefully my teeth aren't too bad.

In the midst of this—I am learning how to live. I went out this weekend and had fun! I'm realizing that it's okay to make friends at work and at school.

December 7, 2005

I weighed myself last night. I feel great, like I'm back where I should be. Hopefully I can lose the three little pounds I wanted to by the end of the week!

Today I ate all I am going to. It's only 2:00 p.m. but I'll make it. I'll work out extra hard too.

So, last week at work, "Lindsey" told me she was raped. It scared me, because that is my fear and I've never known anyone who had it happen to them. She was drunk, but I still feel so bad. She seemed to be okay and is thankful that she wasn't injured, killed, etc. That was so encouraging to me because I would not be so together and have a positive attitude after going through something so awful. I admire her strength. "Natalie" told me about her thyroid problem last week and how she has to be on medication and her hair was falling out. Then I also found out a woman from church has cancer. Maybe God is trying to teach me something

January 17, 2006

So, I'm back at school. My breaks are long but I actually don't mind it that much. I just worked out burning off 400 calories. Yay! I ate a few pretzels and a Slim Fast bar. Yesterday, I did great. I only had a Slim Fast bar, then a smoothie for lunch. But after work, I had to go and eat pretzels, but I didn't eat the whole bag like I usually do when I binge/purge. I threw up two or three times. I felt bad because I knew Stacy could hear me. But once again—did she try to stop me? Nope. So why should I care if she knows or not!?! I know I'm probably a hard person to live with now but hey, it's not easy for me either. I think I resent her for losing so much weight, as terrible as it sounds. Like she accomplished what I cannot. I'm still going to diet though, it's obviously working, whatever I'm doing. I wish I could cry. I hate this numbness. But how can I ask for help for something I don't want to give up and I'm not convinced is that big of a deal!?! Who would I ask? I don't even know where to go or what to do. Maybe I'll find it. Maybe it will come to me. Maybe it will be forced on me. Maybe I will get worse before I get better.

January 19, 2006

I hate school! I hate it! I just want to quit. I so do not want to be here, although I really don't want to be at work either. I've been eating too much lately. Yesterday at The Cheesecake Factory, I ate part of my sandwich, soup, and salad at lunch and no cheesecake. ☺ That's all I had, but today I ate a lot of pretzels for breakfast. I was so hungry. Oh well, I can't eat anymore. It's 2:30 now and I can't eat after 7:00 anymore. I'll go to class, work out, go home, and NOT eat. I can do it. I have to keep losing. I already feel like a failure, just feeling fat and lazy with no control over what I eat! I can be in control! I'll get it back.

January 22, 2006

I threw up probably 20 times today. What is my problem? Why can't I stop!?! I thought Rachel hated me. I don't know why she wouldn't because I haven't been very nice to her, but she gave me a card yesterday that was so nice I almost cried. I know I need to get help. I don't want it and I don't really even think I can do it. But I know that I have to or I'll die. Maybe not right away, maybe not even physically, but spiritually, I'm dead. Emotionally…mentally…socially. I was so shocked that she actually still cares. I'm happy she does, though. I just wish I could find the right person to help. And I wish I could cry! I want to be upset. I want to cry my eyes out. If I feel sad and emotional maybe I'll realize I have a huge problem.

I know it is ridiculous, throwing up 10 to 20 times a day almost everyday the past two weeks! When did it get to that?!? I know I might not look bad but I can see a difference in my body. My hair is so thin and breaking and I'm freezing all the time, and sometimes I look at myself and I don't see me.

I want to find someone to help, to listen, to care, to love me. I hate the fact that I wrote the letter to Rachel. It was to talk myself into thinking I'm okay and don't need help. It's not to convince her; obviously she can tell I'm only fooling myself.

healthy and deal with my problems. I wish I had the desire to go into it with passion and motivation to conquer this disease. I like challenges, and I need to view it as that. A challenge I can overcome. I guess I just can't stop because my body is addicted and I love it too much. Throwing up does give me such a high; I need it daily to function. It makes me feel so energetic and good. Why is it though that one minute I feel so good but the same thing makes me so sad!?! If only I can change my views and be determined to get better!

What I ate today...and threw up:

Starbucks (frappucino), soup & ½ sandwich, 1 roll, 1 cookie, ½ bag of pretzels , ½ bag chocolate chips, 1 package dried fruit, 4 Pop Tarts

April 15, 2006

All I ate, binged, and purged:

2 frappucinos, cookie, 1 big bag of M&Ms, pretzels

April 17, 2006

All I ate today, and once again, purged:

2 Pop Tarts, 1 candy bar, lots of ice cream, frappucino, 2 big cookies (400 calories each...), box of Oreos, more ice cream, 10 pretzel rods, ½ bag gummi bears = approximately 4770 calories.

Throwing up equals success (in my mind).

Eating equals no success.

April 23, 2006

I finally got things right with my parents, Stacy, and Rachel. I apologized for acting immature. It was something that I needed to do, and I'm glad I did. I really need to view my eating disorder as a challenge. I need to view it as something to conquer, because that is the only way I get things accomplished. I'm so embarrassed. I can't even eat one thing pleasurable in two weeks—my assignment for counseling. I'm not even trying which is stupid when I think about it, because I'm paying someone to help me, and I'm not even listening to her. I want to give up. I really don't care anymore. I really wish I could have someone to walk through this by my side. That would make it easier. As much as I hate to admit it, I like my eating disorder for the attention it gives me. I do get annoyed at people getting in my business and everything about what I eat, but I also love it when they notice I've lost weight. Friday someone asked me and hopefully more people will notice next weekend.

Anyways, I do like the attention even if it's for a negative thing. I don't want the people to care that do and I want the people that don't care to care or notice. It's my thing that people know about me and I don't want that to disappear.

April 27, 2006

I really don't know what's wrong with me and I wish I could figure it out. It's almost like I feel like two completely different people. There's a part of me that knows how badly I need help, and I think I want it. I want to put 100% effort into getting better, getting closer to God, living my life, and not hurting my body. I want this but at the same time I absolutely don't want to change anything. I don't want to try, and the last thing I want to do is pray or read the Bible. I guess I don't want to give it up, even though I know I'll be happier. I still feel like going to counseling or "getting help" in whatever way is giving into what everyone wanted and

May 2, 2006

I finally yelled at my dad. He made me so mad, trying to lecture me on my future choices. I hate how he tries to change my mind when I make a decision. It makes me furious. Not only the fact that he does that but denies it. I've never been so mad at my parents. I just want my dad to acknowledge that I feel controlled. He doesn't have to agree—just acknowledge it and apologize. I hate not having anyone to talk to. I feel so alone. I am alone.

May 10, 2006

I went to counseling today and I feel guilty for not being completely honest. I am paying $100 a session ($50 technically with insurance) for help, and I am not even being honest about everything. I haven't eaten since Sunday. I don't want to and even though it makes me feel good, I don't want to tell anyone about it. Today was the first time I can thing of that someone pointed out that food controlled me. And I see it, to an extent.

What Sharon is good at:
- *Gymnastics/coaching*
- *Running*
- *School/good grades*
- *Making smoothies*
- *Scrapbooking*
- *Being goofy and sarcastic*
- *Bargain shopping*
- *Reading and comprehending*
- *Thinking outside the box*
- *Making new friends*
- *Writing*
- *Being productive*

- *Being spontaneous*
- *Dancing*
- *Juggling*
- *Cleaning*

May 12, 2006

I like Victoria because she is really nice, but not too nice. We click well, and I'm glad I can talk to her! I ate today at work because I felt like I should. I hadn't eaten all week and all I had was a salad and half a piece of cake but I felt so sick after and all I wanted to do was throw up.

May 14, 2006

I finally got motivated enough to move today. I was glad to be out of my apartment but it was sad at the same time. I just keep telling myself that it will be an adjustment of course but it will be okay. Every other time my living situation changed it was hard but I got used to it. I had to eat dinner with my family today and I was sooo stressed about it! It was almost scary to me how much I dreaded it. Then I actually had to eat and I literally hated it. I barely ate anything but I felt guilty and like a failure and I hate my family and I just wanted to go home. I'm upset with my body and myself and upset for what happened at work on Saturday and not saying anything. I feel so stupid for lying at counseling. It's such a waste of time if I try to hide my problems. I think I've been trying to fool other people into thinking I'm okay and I really don't have a problem (or at least that it's not that big of a deal). But obviously it is. I'm even fooling myself by acting like it's not that huge of a problem. When I was so scared today about eating and everything I realized how into this I am. Being dishonest or lying to myself is just hurting me more.

May 15, 2006

I realize how extreme I am in food and what I am doing. I guess if I throw up anything I eat or even drink with calories I definitely have a problem. I seem to think it's normal, or think it is okay. I know my problem is bigger than I am admitting to myself or anyone else. Throwing up drinks or salad is crazy. But I do have hope. I will get better, slowly, but one day.

May 16, 2006

I went to my Ireland class today and actually enjoyed it. I'm a dork I guess and I like learning. The teacher is so nice and cool so I'm really excited! Then, I went to counseling. It always amazes me that I can think I'm okay then I can't stop crying when I talk about things, because I'm really hurting. I am becoming much more open and sharing my feelings and everything, which is good. It is still really hard but I can do it because I know it helps. Saying that I lied and wanted to be honest really was a brave step. I don't want to be fake or try to impress Victoria. She knows I'm not perfect. I asked her if she believed me that I had a problem and she said yes, and that I hide it well. I don't know why, but I had to hear that, because I get the vibe from some of my friends that they don't seem to care or think it's that big of a deal. So we talked about how I ate on Sunday and was planning on not eating today but I did. I started crying just thinking about how I let myself down, just by eating one chicken taco and an apple. I wanted to throw up so badly but I didn't and I couldn't take the stress, but I was so glad to be able to talk to someone. I felt guilty and like a failure for not making it all day without eating. I knew that I would probably come home and binge and purge or throw up whatever I could. I was totally set on doing it, even though I tried to imagine tonight turning out differently. I said I would call a friend but I didn't think that would really work. On a scale of one to ten, I said I was a nine of certainty that I would binge/purge. It was all I wanted to do, but God is faithful and will always provide a way out (1 Corinthians 10:13).

I was thinking about what keeps me coming back to counseling. I know now it is God. So, I drove to work to pick up my tip money and didn't want to leave, so I talked to two friends there (no one I called picked up). Then I came back home. I talked to "Katharine" and she tried to talk me out of being stressed and that didn't work either but I didn't give up. Then Josh and Amy left to go for a walk and I started writing. I am okay. Everything was against me tonight, but I fought through it. God definitely helped me. Thank you God, for being my strength.

Sometimes I wish Victoria could just follow me around and help me make the right decisions all day. But when I leave her office I'm alone in the world and I have to face it by myself. I can decide what I want to do. She can only help me to think through things while I'm there. But I appreciate her love and concern so much. I feel like I don't get that from many people.

I got three A's and two A-'s this semester, and I was actually upset, even though my GPA was a 3.884 and my cumulative is a 3.75 or something. I felt stupid for getting the one A- because I had so much extra credit in my Drug Use class and I felt like I would have to be an idiot to not and like my body better. Even though I might not absolutely love my body (I still want to lose weight) at least I like it more than when I gain weight and eat. I hate eating. It doesn't make me feel good. I know it's right and healthy and what I need but it makes me feel terrible. Why would I want to change from something that makes me feel good to something that makes me hate myself more? I guess I hate myself on both sides. I just haven't had a positive experience eating in such a long time that nothing makes me want to do it. I really wish I had someone to help me out. Victoria is good to talk to but I only see her once a week. God, please bring someone into my life on a daily basis to help me. I'll never recover alone. I am sure of that.

I know I'm going to hate going back to work. I'm going to work a lot. I have to and want to make money but I don't know how I'm going to deal with it. I hope I find a new job ASAP. I hate that place. I hate those people. I hate it! I hate it! I hate it!!!

June 3, 2006

I finally got on this plane after waiting for seven hours in the airport! I can't wait to be home because no one will be surprised or try to get me to eat if I don't eat there. I became better at purging in public, in the restaurants and even in the hotel while my roommates were there. I've never done that before except for living with Stacy and she knew so I guess I just didn't care. I got better at not eating at meals and making it look like I ate when I didn't. I'm so uncomfortable around food and eating in front of people. I dread eating! I hate it! Nothing ever sounds appealing and that which does I end up throwing up. I know I can't have candy and stuff around because I'll just binge on it (little or big binges). So one would think that I should buy small amounts or just get dessert when I go out to eat or something but that obviously doesn't work either way unless someone eats with me and follows me around after. I'm getting so good at it, it's scaring me. I can see myself throwing up at work now or anywhere. I'm so scared to go back Monday. Oh well, I guess whatever happens will be okay. God knows what he's doing.

June 4, 2006

I'm actually sad not being in Ireland! I really loved it and I miss it. So glad that I got to go though, and actually experience it!

Last night my messages were crazy to come home to. I truly do have wonderful friends though. I'm hurt by what happened with everyone at work not believing me, but I'm glad I was gone for the past two weeks. At least I didn't have to deal with it. I'm not too scared to go back, but I hope I don't really have to. It might be miserable. I really don't regret what I did because I did nothing wrong! I did the right thing and handled the situation professionally. What people say, and if they gossip and criticize, I can't help that. They obviously don't know how I feel or what went on. It still hurts that they don't and won't take into consideration how I felt violated and uncomfortable!

God, I feel like Christians are constantly letting me down. Actually more than that, they're crushing me. I know they're just human and I forgive them. But, I'm still hurt. I know you can heal my hurt and renew me with joy. God, I love you and I feel you. I don't try to get away from Christianity even though I feel like others turn me off to it, because I have a special relationship with you. I do. I can parents, and I lived with her, and wanted her to be able to help me. This session was the start of a life-changing week. Victoria knew what I was doing and that it was going on for at least a month, and she told me I needed to see a doctor that week. I told her I probably wouldn't, because I was at an okay weight still and I didn't think it was that big of an issue. But after talking with them, I was scared of the health risks and somehow the hospital got brought up. I wanted to get it over with, and so I said I would go to get everything checked out. I never like to make drastic decisions, and I kind of thought it was a little extreme, but both of them assured me it wasn't, and they were extremely worried about me.

At the hospital, I found out my electrolytes were okay and the doctor didn't think anything was wrong with me. It was like she didn't believe me that I had a problem, even though I told her my behaviors and that I had lost about twenty pounds pretty rapidly. She told me that I didn't look like I had an eating disorder, and that my teeth weren't "that bad." I was so hurt, and confused. I had spent close to three years hiding my problem, and now that I wanted help, I had to convince people that I did indeed have an eating disorder. I was thankful I was physically okay but frustrated that no one would help. I simply was told I was dehydrated, received fluids through an IV, and then was sent home, without any advice to maybe eat something, or to keep drinking fluids.

I was hopeless when I walked out of there, feeling stupid that nothing was wrong, like a failure even at my eating disorder, and wishing I would have been admitted, because at least then I would be getting help. Amy called an outpatient facility later that day, which was three days a week for three hours. After hearing about my history, they said I was too severe and would have to be eating meals and farther along in recovery. I was crushed because I felt like once again I failed…two hospitals wouldn't even take me. Plus I was receiving mixed messages, that I really wasn't bad at all, then too sick for another place. Amy called every hospital around but none had a program. I was so depressed, because everyone had always told me to get help, and I thought help was supposed to be easy to get.

I became suicidal in the next day or so, wanting it all to be over. I was hopeless and just wanted to die. I don't know if I would have actually carried anything out, but I was terrified of my thoughts that kept me awake all night, and afraid I would do something stupid. I went back to another hospital and was admitted in the psychiatric unit. I wanted to leave immediately and only talked myself into staying because my roommate came in and was normal and cool. She was a younger woman, with post-partum depression. We were able to talk and relate to each other's battle with depression. Also, she was a Christian. Once again God had come through and provided. I stayed there for two days, and got mentally stable again. I didn't get the help I needed with my eating disorder, and I didn't even try to eat or keep anything down. I talked to a dietician one day, but no one forced me to eat, or cared what I did after I did take two bites.

After arriving home and discussing my options with my parents and Victoria, I flew to Remuda Ranch, a Christian eating disorder treatment facility in Arizona, just a few days later. I never once thought I would end up at a place like that. I was in denial so long that my

I think it's so weird that I weigh a lot less than I did, but I don't see myself as thin. I honestly don't want to look too sick. But Kelly who has told me in the past that if I lost 10 more pounds I would look sick, now that I have says she is jealous that I'm so skinny. I almost want to get worse and everything just to make my parents feel bad.

June 9, 2006

Ireland was such a good thing for me even though I feel like I failed in so many ways. I became so aware of how unhappy my eating disorder makes me. I don't experience life in the way that I should.

June 11, 2006

I am so hard on myself and don't allow myself to look at the good in my life. It's almost like I don't want myself to succeed if it's not 100%.

Successes in Ireland…major & minor:

- *Drinking juice (drinks with calories)*
- *Eating breakfast and not purging everyday*
- *Sometimes eating something small for lunch (even if it was small)*
- *Trying new foods*
- *Eating dinner and not purging a few nights, then eating breakfast the next day (not starving to make up for it)*
- *Going a day without excessive exercise*
- *Being myself around others*
- *Allowing others to get to know me*
- *Calling home or a friend when I needed to (in the airport on the way home)*

- *Not blowing money on a bunch of food to binge on*
- *Sometimes eating dessert and not purging*
- *Eating fruit, carbs, protein, vegetables, dairy*

God,

Thank you so much for Amy and for the time we spent together last night. We had a misunderstanding but that stuff happens and I'm glad we got to talk. I knew that I wouldn't have had a good time if I went out, so I'm glad I didn't go. I needed to talk to someone who cares about me. I pray that she won't be stressed because of me. I hate being a burden to people. Please help my mom also. I'm so worried about her and I feel so bad that she feels this way. It's all my fault. Please comfort her. You are wonderful. Amen.

June 14, 2006

I actually feel more depressed today than I have in a long time. I knew I had to eat something because I haven't had food since the Sunday I came home. I prayed and God answered my prayer for someone to be home. Josh was here and so that was cool. I ate a salad and a piece of bread. It wasn't much at all but I hated myself for it. I knew I did the right thing but I felt sick after eating and wanted to get rid of it. Earlier today I was starving and ate some yogurt and ended up throwing up. That's insane! I can't even eat two spoonfuls of yogurt. I feel like I've had zero success today. I went to Starbucks with a friend and just ended up throwing up my dinner there.

Why am I so completely torn? God, you promise to help me and heal and be with me, but I can't do anything *right! Why don't you help me? I wish I could think clearly. I wish I would be able to eat. I feel like I've dealt with this for so long and you just won't take it away. Why?!? Why do you keep providing so many people who care about me, but don't change me? Why do I waste my time in counseling? I seriously don't think I will ever be better God. If I am one day, it will be a miracle. I'm so hopeless right now and I don't even want to change.*

I guess any progress I have made is erased. As much as I want to not be sad and hurting my body and ruining my life, there's such a huge part of me that loves this disorder. I just want to keep losing more weight. I want to be skinny. I don't want to eat and if I'm forced to, I'll just throw it up. I don't want to go back to counseling next week. I want to give up.

June 15, 2006

On the phone I told Victoria that I did well yesterday and ate a salad and everything. I lie so much that I didn't even realize I had until I hung up. I failed to mention that I threw up later. Oh and that I didn't ever want to come back to counseling again. I guess Amy is going to come next week to discuss how she can help but what good will it do if I don't want her to?!? It's a good idea and sounds logical but I'm so not at that point to have help or accountability by someone else. I don't want to change! I feel like I'm back at square one.

I still weigh 120 but I feel soo fat! I want to starve tomorrow and lose five pounds by next Wednesday. I've gotten this far so what's five more?

June 16, 2006

Today I asked a friend at work if she thought that counseling is worth it for me if I'm not set on changing, and if I don't even want help. She said that it's like an addiction, and I should look at it like someone with a drug or alcohol problem. They still might crave the drug but they shouldn't stop going to rehab. I thought that was a good point.

I thought about it, and it's true. Nothing bad is happening because of me going. I guess I'm more emotional but that's not necessarily a bad thing. At least I'm learning how to deal with my feelings and problems, rather than shoving them aside. She also pointed out that I do want help at some points. It goes up and down, but I shouldn't give up just because I don't want it at a certain time in my life.

I wish I didn't have such drastic ups and downs, but I guess I'm just normal. On the way home from counseling the other day, I was really excited to try to eat and make progress. I was all about making a book of verses and quotes to encourage me when I needed it. Then I got home and after I actually did eat I got so upset with myself. I talked myself into never coming back to counseling again, and convincing myself to starve again (and purge). I didn't even really pay attention during counseling because I was too distracted by my hunger and wondering when the next time I would eat would be. But it's so frustrating how I can go from a total extreme of being all excited about getting help and being healthy to convincing myself I'm fine and don't need it.

I do want to be successful though and have a good story to tell people. One day I want to talk to the girls at the YMCA where I did gymnastics. I want to talk to them now, even, and tell them it's not worth it. I don't want other people to go through what I am going through. I never really if I don't have anything better to do! What is with people? The worst thing is not being believed! Especially over huge things...

June 23, 2006

I slept for like four hours on the couch and then woke up and now I can't sleep. I am so incredibly frustrated and confused. I always thought that getting help would be the easy part. Getting help is supposed to be easy! When someone wants it, they should be able to get it. It's like I have spend the past three years convincing everyone and myself that I didn't have a problem and now I have to convince everyone that I do.

I wish I felt the same way I felt on Wednesday. I was just so ready to get help and wanted to be taken care of. I'm glad that I am okay and everything, but I really wanted help immediately. The more time that goes by, the more I don't even want it anymore and that scares me. It makes me feel like a failure too. I can't even get help for an eating disorder. Hospitals keep rejecting me! Why is it that when I finally want help, no one will help me get it?!? It's so ridiculously backwards. I also feel like I can't even hurt my body. It's like I fail at having an eating disorder. I really don't want my body to be hurt, but I think if it were, then getting help would be easier.

I can't believe that I've lost twenty pounds in the most extremely unhealthy ways. I don't care what my electrolytes are! I can't eat!!!! I did have a smoothie today and for dinner I had like two crackers and two bites of soup. I thought I'd be okay when Josh and Amy left but I wasn't. I thought drinking a glass of milk would be healthy so I did, and then I thought, "That was too many calories," so I threw up. I hate it! I can't even drink anything. I would have thrown up the smoothie if I were alone. It took everything in me to eat a little bit of soup, I hated it and didn't want it and hated myself for eating it. It's not like I'm trying to make myself worse but I feel like I am.

The more I'm asked if I'm thinking of hurting myself, the more I actually do. I feel like I'm going crazy when I am asked that. Last night I drove to get a movie and looked down for a minute and swerved into the left lane. I was like, "Whoa, good thing there wasn't a car coming." But then I thought, "I wish I did get in an accident." I guess I do think of hurting myself even if I don't think I ever will. I wish I would get hurt and have to go to the hospital. I think that's why I threw up last night and now I'm determined not to eat. I don't want to live. I don't want to live at all, but I don't want to die! I really don't. I just want to feel good. I don't want to feel like this anymore. I wish I had someone to talk to. I'm always so alone and it makes me worse. God, help me. I'm so sorry for feeling this way. I wish I could feel love and be at peace with you. I feel like a bad person for not being able to let you take away my pain. Please help me. If I need to, give me the strength to tell someone how I really feel.

Later that day:

I feel like I should be at work if I'm not in the hospital. I do feel extremely guilty for not being there. But I realized today that I wouldn't be able to function. That scares me so much. I don't want to do anything. The thing that I hate is that I don't even have a reason to feel this way.

I just figured out why I would rather be in an inpatient program rather than outpatient. If I'm there for a while I can focus and won't worry about coming home and eating needed something. I remember praying for help and the next day Stacy called my parents. It was exactly not what I had planned or how I wanted it but it is what happened. Then I prayed while crying hysterically Friday morning. I was so scared that I might hurt myself. You provided this place for me at the perfect time. Thank you for answering my cry for help. I still have such a long road before me. It's so hard but I know that it will be okay with you by my side. I know now I don't need to try to save myself. You will. Please continue to strengthen me. Be my strong tower, my love, and my life. I am nothing without you. I have learned this and seen it. I need you! Amen.

4:50 p.m.

I don't know what I'm going to do when I get out of here but the beauty of it is that I don't have to. I know for sure that I'm probably going to quit my job. I really don't need that stress and I know that's all it would be. I don't need to worry about where I'll work. I'm finally realizing that this is about life and death and I want to live!!! I not only want to live, but live a full and abundant life. And continuing on like this, physically all right or not, is not what I want. It's so hard for me to stand back and look at myself and see how bad I really am. Sometimes I wonder if I'm bad enough for something like Remuda Ranch (for $100,000!) or even another outpatient thing in another state. I know that it would be worth it. I can't keep food down! I really don't want someone to have to watch me use the bathroom or check the toilet but if that's what has to happen, then that's what has to happen. I want to get better!

Having other people is wonderful and I'm glad I trust people like Victoria and Amy. Having people who know me, notice that I'm a lot worse really fast, shows that it's really bad even if I can't see it. I am scared to have to find a new job, and possibly leave for three months, and take a semester off of school, and not live in Kent, but that may be the best. I am almost willing to do anything it takes. Going away would be scary but probably the best. I guess God will work things out. All I have to do is trust him.

I just realized that before, I admitted I had a problem (when everything came out, Stacy told my parents, I started going to counseling), but I didn't admit I needed help until yesterday. Even Wednesday, I willingly went to the ER and knew I had to do something before I got worse, but I didn't really admit I needed to go to a treatment facility. Knowing I need help and wanting it is a huge step in the right direction. Today was easier than yesterday. Tomorrow will be even better. Eating hasn't been easy for me, but I guess this time is for me to focus on the depression and thinking straight again.

What I ate today:
2 bites of egg—purged
5 grapes
3 carrot sticks
2 cucumber slices
½ of a grilled chicken Caesar salad—purged
¼ c frozen yogurt

June 26, 2006
Heavenly Father,

I come to you in great need. I'm so uncertain about my future. I trust you even though it's hard. Please work everything out. Please help me not to worry. I have you and know that you will take care of me. I want to ask so many big things of you, but I am afraid to ask, because I honestly *don't think they are possible. I'm so sorry for not believing you are able to do anything. Please forgive me. I know you can because you have done so much already. God, I'm so worried but I can't be anymore. Give me the peace I had even earlier today. Help me not to be scared about money. You have everything in control. Lord, you've always answered my prayers before, so why wouldn't you now? I want to give these things to you—they are all so big—but you are so much bigger than any problem and are so in control of my life!*

First of all, please let me be placed into the treatment center where you want me to be. I am willing to go wherever. Please tear down any barriers, such as money, or distance, or time. Please guide us in the right direction and let me be in the perfect place for me. I believe you can do anything, and I believe you could provide $100,000 for it tomorrow. I'm not even asking you to but I know and believe wholeheartedly you are able. I just ask that I will be able to go where you want me to, and where I would receive the best help.

Also, I pray about the insurance and going back to school for a few classes in the fall. I know my parents are very worried about the time, and getting back to school in the fall, as "dropping out" is not an option. You know my needs, and you will provide! I am so sure of that. I ask that whatever happens with the insurance and going back to school or not, that it will work out. I really do trust you because I have no control.

I do know that the treatment and getting better is my first priority and I wish it were my parents'! I feel that it all comes down to the money. In the hospital on Saturday, it was all about doing whatever and how they really wanted to see me better. Now I feel like they are thinking cheapest, closest, and quickest. In regards to the treatment center, what I really want it to be is the best help for me, and what God wants!

Please show my parents this. Do a miracle. I've never asked you for a miracle but I have more faith than ever that you can do one now! Lastly, please help my roommate situation to work out! If my roommate could find someone to live with the first semester that would be amazing so I wouldn't worry about paying. I don't know what will happen, God...please do whatever. I do trust you, I really do! Amen.

thought I was at the point where I was unhealthy and sick enough to need this much help. I keep convincing myself I'm not that bad since I still see myself as fat. Anyways, she said I had lost a lot of weight, which I thought I was hiding from her for some dumb reason. I didn't think she noticed since she didn't say anything. She also said she thought I definitely need inpatient care. Just hearing that made me feel better, but I'm not sure exactly why. I trust her, and know she needed to push me in the right direction. I'm excited to be going, but also scared, and afraid of how I'll have to change. I do want to continue on like this because I love it and I love the way I look. Victoria pointed out that I didn't really want to come to counseling, and I went for everyone else, but now I go for myself. The important thing is that I kept coming and let God bring me to where I am. I am doing the same thing now, I'm kind of going for myself, but mostly for everyone else, and fear of letting them down. But God can change me. He can do the impossible. He already has. Just the fact that I got to this point from last week with all the obstacles is a miracle. He has brought me too far just to "drop me on my head" (Victoria). ☺

God,

Please be with me these next 45 days. I'm so scared and I can't do it alone. I don't really know what to pray so I just ask that you will do the unthinkable. I have hope! You will rescue me. I trust you to provide exactly what I need. Thank you for continually giving me the best, I really don't deserve this. Amen.

July 2, 2006

I'm finally here, and have spent 1½ very long days at Remuda Ranch. I have been doing well; I actually haven't *really been able to cry since I've got here. I wish it were easier for me to open up and get to know the girls and really want to get better. I really don't want to give up my eating disorder. At first I came in yesterday wanting to "perform" like always. I did it in the beginning of counseling and I felt the same exact way yesterday. So I ate all my food to please the people monitoring. But that does no good. I have to choose to eat and be healthy because I want to take care of my body. Today I didn't like the breakfast and didn't want it, so I took the supplement instead. But I couldn't even continue on without perfection at lunch and dinner. I hate that everyone is like, "Oh, you're doing so well! Good job!" Just because they see me eat...I just really want to throw the food in their faces and scream. I may be eating but only as little as possible and only because I feel like I have to. I wish someone could just see inside my mind and understand how much of a struggle I'm in. I am so scared of food. The temptation to binge isn't there anymore, but all I want to do is puke after I eat anything. I've been dehydrated ever since I've arrived here because I don't even feel like drinking. All I seem to do is compare myself to the other girls. I'm glad I'm not as sick as some physically are, but my head is screwed up probably more I think. I hate being here because I feel like I'm only here to "perform" like I should impress everyone and complete the program—then I'll go home and immediately lose any weight I've gained and go back to starving myself. I don't really want to, but I see myself doing that. But, there's a small part of me that sees myself happy with my body, myself, and successful in recovery. All I've done today was sit around and think. That was draining. I'm convinced I'm still relatively healthy from living on Slim Fast bars.... at least they have vitamins and calories. It's better than* nothing I guess. The doctor did say I had malnutrition, dehydration, and slight electrolyte imbalances. At the rate I was descending, though, I got bad fast and would have only gotten worse. Eating sucks, and that part is crappy. So are the rules, and being away from home. I woke up today thinking about how much I didn't want to be here and everything, but then I gave myself a pep talk and thought, "Sharon, it's not supposed to be fun." I didn't come here on vacation or to have a great time. I came so I wouldn't die. And getting better is hard work and a lot of pressure. I can't do it alone. I need a lot of help and I'm learning that is okay.

God,

I know you brought me here but I still can't say that I'm happy I'm here. I want so badly to do the right thing but I also want to hold onto my eating disorder. I pray that you will help me and be with me because I feel so alone. Please help my family not to worry about me, and let us have a great time when they come at the end of the month. Help me to figure things out. I am driving myself crazy thinking about things. Let me focus on you. I love you. I wish I were near to you! Amen.

July 3, 2006

I realized today that I came into here thinking that I will just start eating again…and be monitored so I don't throw up, and then I'll be all better and get out and be healthy. But the more I think about it, the truth is, eating my meals and attending the classes isn't going to make me recover successfully. I have to deal with my issues behind it. I'm more aware at how much of a mental problem this is, and how I need to fix it to really get better. My behaviors *are important to eliminate but I've got to get past this "good girl" attitude of clearing my plate and doing what everyone says, to really getting past whatever is making me do this and wanting to get better. I hate wanting help for so long and wanting to come here and everything, yet I keep imagining myself going home still holding onto my eating disorder and the body I have now, and going back to how I was before I came. And that's scary and makes me depressed, like I'm wasting my time.*

I met with the dietician "Katie" today and she was very nice. I liked talking to her about my eating habits and being honest with someone. But having to gain weight scares the hell out of me. I just want to start eating healthy and let my body adjust. Having to drink Boost scares me so much, so I hope I don't have to. My thinking is that I would just go home and restrict and purge until I lose any weight I gain.

I know that even though I'm not under 100 pounds or anything, I'm still at the point of the other anorexics here. They still have to gain weight to be at a healthy and natural weight, and probably so will I. I wish I would be more willing and less afraid. I pray God that you will help me as I eat lunch. I need your help. Please heal my body and let this process be natural and easy to accept. Please help my parents not to worry and may we talk a lot tonight and share our lives. I love you, God—please bless the rest of this day. Amen.

July 4, 2006

Today we don't have the program since it's a holiday, which means some more sitting around and doing some pointless activities. The days drag on and I feel like they'll never end. I can't imagine ever getting out of here.

August 15th sounds so far away. If I went home today, I would definitely go back to my old habits and lose any weight I've gained here, and probably more.

I just ate breakfast, and I feel so disgusting. I am mad at myself, which doesn't even really make sense. I am so used to not eating that when I do it's the opposite of what I want to do and think I should be doing so I feel like a failure. I am a failure. This place doesn't seem to be helping me, I feel like I'm just worse in my stubbornness. I want to leave. I want to be better but I am scared of the process. I want this to be worth it, but I honestly don't have too much hope for the end.

Dear Heavenly Father,

I am so weary. I don't have any hope. Where did my positive outlook and sense of hope in recovery go? I came here with a really good attitude but now I can't seem to keep it. I feel hopeless again. I need you to get me through. Amen.

July 5, 2006

I feel better today. Sometimes all I need is some time by myself to think about everything and process my feelings. After talking to my family the first time I cooled down a bit and was able to talk with them again later. I feel so hopeless at times and positive at others. I hope the hopeful times and thoughts start coming more often, before I give up. I wanted to go home so badly yesterday before Chapel. Then I remembered why I was here and not in an outpatient program. I can't leave since I'm in Arizona. If all that is keeping me here is the fact that I can't leave, then that's all I need. God knew what he was doing by providing me the ability to come here. It's frustrating and it's hard but that's why I'm here. If it were easy to recover on my own, I would be doing it at home. But I need a lot of help. When I got my body compositions done the other day, I realized that maybe my view of my body is really distorted. I didn't really believe anyone when they said, "You don't have anything left to lose." I kept thinking I was so fat, but when the lady tried to measure it, she couldn't really get any and said how muscular I was. I thought, "Hmmm maybe I don't have much to lose, and it's okay to have muscle." I can't see myself viewing myself as okay if I gain weight, but at least I can admit that I see myself in a distorted way now.

July 6, 2006

I feel like I ate a ton of food for breakfast—an orange, 2 pieces of toast WITH BUTTER, and scrambled eggs. It is a lot compared to what I normally eat. But that's okay, it's going to be hard. I just really hate the fact that I have to start eating more, at snack time and everything. I have to have 6-7 EQ's now (equivalents; basically 600-700 calories in snacks), which is scary. I'll only have 6 for sure. I'm still holding onto my eating disorder in that way. I'm so afraid of gaining weight. I don't understand why I have to since I'm at a healthy weight. I am physically healthy so that makes I even harder. I'm so thankful I am okay, but it's so hard to accept the fact that I can still gain some weight and look good and be healthy. It's such a stinkin' battle. I keep thinking that if I do gain too much, I'll just go home and lose it, but I don't want to relapse. I wish Katie would realize it's okay for me to be small and I probably don't have to weigh as much as I used to. I hated myself when I weighed a lot more before and it won't be any different if I gain it back again. I would just starve and purge what I eat until I'm back at a weight I want to be.

Things that I miss:
- *Starbucks*
- *Playing with Zeke (my nephew)*
- *Watching "Friends" episodes*
- *E-mail*
- *Gum*
- *My bed & blankets*
- *Razors*
- *Skim milk*
- *Smoothies*
- *Family & friends*
- *Driving my car*
- *Victoria*
- *My cell phone*
- *Sleeping in*
- *Running*
- *Going to bed late*
- *Music*
- *Reading books of my choice*

"We are all imperfect, and that's perfectly okay." -A fellow Remuda Ranch friend

July 7, 2006

It's hard to believe that I actually have been here a week. I made it! When I think about the 5½ remaining weeks it's depressing. But hopefully it will go fast. I don't really know what my problem is here, but I feel like I can't feel my emotions as strongly as at home. I'm just going through the motions, eating the food, sometimes purging, going to appointments, groups, therapy, and the stupid activities. All I look forward to is sleep. Or being able to talk on the phone. Then last night my mom and I sorta had a fight. I try to be open and express my feelings to her in an honest way. But instead of just acknowledging how I feel, she has to try to talk me out of my feelings. She doesn't understand how awful I feel. She doesn't have this problem! She doesn't get that I feel sick from having to eat so much, and then feel depressed from sitting around doing nothing. And the loneliness from having no close friends. And the frustration of wanting so badly to be able to open up to someone, yet pushing away those who try. And the constant battle in my head of wanting to recover yet wanting to continue on like this, and having every intention as of right now to go home and lose any weight I've gained. I don't want to have an eating disorder. I really don't. Or maybe I wish I just never had one. I see some of the workers here who haven't struggled with one, and I try to imagine their lives not in bondage to food. I mean I know they have issues too but I wish I had that ease in regards to food and my body. I hate my body—my body image seems to be getting worse.

Anyways, I don't want anyone to tell me, "Oh just do what they say. They know what they're doing." No shit! They're professionals and have a high success rate of recovery and I know that. But it doesn't take away my anxiety about food and the self-hatred while I eat and after I eat, and the unbearable urges to throw up after eating or go running or not eat for days. It disgusts me that I ate so much. All I think about is food and dread the next time I have to eat. I'm never even hungry, because the snacks are so often in between meals. And when I'm not eating I'm trying to plan my snacks so that I get the least amount of calories. AHHH!!! I can't stop being obsessed with it. The therapy is helpful I guess but I still don't know how I'll address the issues I don't even feel emotions about. I feel so screwed up.

July 8, 2006

I can't believe I'm starting my 2nd week here. It's still hard to believe I'm here. I don't feel like I've made much progress even though people are telling me I have. "Sara" [my therapist] said yesterday that I'm right were I should be, even in my state of confusion, which I feel is a failure. I guess I haven't failed yet. Failing would be going home after 45 days here and immediately going back to my old lifestyle. I have such and intense fear of failure but then at other times I feel like it's not even worth trying.

July 9, 2006

Today I had yogurt with granola and raisin cereal for breakfast, which was surprisingly good. The bad part was the peaches and blueberry muffin with disgusting BUTTER I had to have with it. Yuck!!! They always check to make sure we used all the butter. Sheesh. I'm never using butter again when I go home. AND I'm gonna drink skim milk! HA! We just had a community meeting and it was brought up how we're not supposed to write down everything we order. Oh well, I do and I really don't care! There are so many rules here. I love doing anything I'm not supposed to. If I want to see what I have eaten even if it scares me, oh well. I think it's good in a way because I can see what I have eaten and what's healthy. Maybe if I look back and see that I'm not gaining a ton of weight, then I can accept I need to eat that much. For snack in like 10 minute I'm going to have an apple with peanut butter, then yogurt covered *raisins later, then trail mix at night. As much as I do obsess about meals and what I ate all day, I want to try to stop worrying about my meal plan. This week my goal is to let go of my fears of my meal plan and follow it. Not that I haven't been following it, except I have thrown up before bed when my roommates aren't in the room. I only did it like 3 days this week, but didn't even purge that much food. That shows how much of a problem this is in my mind. Like I know I won't lose weight from throwing up a cup of pudding but just the feeling of fullness, and getting it out of my body is so intense I can't relax until I purge.*

July 10, 2006

Song of Solomon 8:7 "Many waters cannot quench love, neither can floods drown it."
Dear God,

Thank you for your awesome love! I am so blessed by you and today I realize that it's true. I want to become more in love with you. Please bring me closer to you in the next few weeks. I know I fail sometimes in expressing my love to you. I forget about you, and I try so hard to beat this on my own, but I've never been successful. So I know I need you, and I cry out to you today. Please help me to not be as afraid of the food as I have been. I pray that you would also help me to be less anxious. Help the new anti-depressants to work, and surround me with calmness. I pray that my family session with my parents will go well and may I be able to express what I'm feeling. I love you and trust you to do a miracle in me here. I'm waiting, patiently. Amen.

July 11, 2006

I feel like I've eaten a ton of food: ½ a bagel, cantaloupe and a mixed berry parfait. It might have actually tasted good if I was just eating one of those things. I hate how I feel after eating. I hate my body worse and myself for having to eat, and not choosing to. Well, I guess I choose, but I still eat for everyone else.

Goals:
- ❑ *Pick what I want to eat when ordering meals on the computer and at snack*
- ❑ *Not to obsess about calories or food labels*
- ❑ *3 Boosts a day—I can do it!*

July 12, 2006

I hate this place sooo much I just want to go home. I really do. But going home would only equal FAILURE! So I feel like I need to stay to please everyone else and my parents, and I feel so guilty for them paying for all of this. I don't feel like anyone listens to me here...doctors, MHT's (mental health technicians), Katie, the girls, even Sara, and the psychiatrist. AHHH! I hate the fact that the stupid rules are inconsistent and the workers don't seem to know what they are. And I don't want to talk to anyone. I really don't. I hate these stupid classes that I have to sit through. I hate eating and I hate drinking Boost. All I want to do after is throw it up. And I love talking to my friends at home because I can open up to them. And I love my parents and don't want everyone telling me I should be mad at them when I'm not. I have told them that I was mad and how I felt in the past. I'm mad at the people here and this shitty ranch. I hate the stupid drama and the hypocritical girls. I hate the fact that I can't relax, and I'm constantly nervous and can't calm down. I hate the stupid long days that start at 5:45 a.m. for no apparent reason. I hate having to be walked somewhere like I'm 10 years old and not being allowed to have cotton balls or face wash in my possession. I hate the 100+ degree weather. I hate the doctor lady that is convinced I have allergies and won't listen to me that I'm actually sick. I hate being away from the people who love me the most. I hate that my parents hurt so badly when I read their letters or talk to them on the phone. I hate having to gain weight. I hate being looked down on by the other girls for not wanting to open up 100% to everyone. And for not being happy or excited about everything…as if I will be here. And finally, I hate the fact that I feel this way!!!!!

I feel so lonely and pissed off at the world. I want to go home, not only because it's so hard here, but also, I honestly don't think this place is all that great ($2000/day). I feel like I have a counselor at home who can help me 1000x more, and I'm sure I could find a dietician I like and who will listen. I don't understand how I can feel one way, like okay about drinking Boost one day and the next day feel completely different. I feel like I'm at a perfectly healthy weight for my height and build, and gaining weight intentionally scares me so much. I really want to just eat and maintain my current weight, because I am happy with it and my body. I don't understand how everyone just says, "Just let it go, don't worry about it," when I obsess about it and it scares the shit out of me. I can't just not feel that way. I really just want to eat normally. I don't want to be unhealthy and I don't want to have an eating disorder. I want to eat healthy and freely, and to trust my body. Not force my body to gain 5 pounds with Boost, when it may or may not do it on its own. I just wish someone would listen to me. I guess Sara sometimes

waste of time, so I felt the need to take a 5-minute shower in order to be more productive that day. I think that will be my equine goal, making the time with Joker a special time for myself and not worrying about food or my eating disorder. I've gone through so many emotions the past 2-3 days. I told Katie how I felt, and it was really hard but she definitely was calm and didn't get mad at me. I was extremely mad and couldn't understand why gaining weight is so vital (I still don't). I know I can refuse the Boost because it is my choice but I'm too stubborn to give up the little control I have such as being able to walk places, having room time, and going out on pass. I guess I can always refuse after my family week if I want to. Maybe I'll like my body, or at least accept it by then. One thing that was pretty stupid on my part was saying to Katie, in regards to intuitive eating, "I'm hungry now and I'm not allowed to eat!" But that was just dumb because she goes, "Then that is a sign your body isn't getting enough." So, that backfired. Great job Sharon.

One thing I keep telling myself is something Victoria said to me once. She said, "If you still want to maintain your weight and eat healthy and watch what you eat, that's great. But at least learn how to do it in a healthy way." And if I do want to be thin and continue being a health nut the rest of my life, it's okay to think that. At least right now and the next 4 weeks I'm learning the right way to do it. And hopefully the urges won't be as strong and I won't worry quite as much as I do now. But giving it ALL up today is too scary, so I have to keep reminding myself of that.

I really want to throw up my Boost. The urge is so incredibly strong. I wish I had gotten to my room earlier so I could've purged before my roommates came. Maybe next time I'll be quicker. I hate this feeling. I know it's not normal to most people but it is to me. How did I ever get so screwed up?!?!

I get so disappointed in myself because I thought I was coming into recovery like, "I want to do this! I'm ready, I'm determined! Bring it on!" When now I am really struggling and can hardly finish a salad and want to give up. And all I do is think about giving up. I'm not even sure if I want to get better most of the time. I hate it here. I hate myself even more for thinking that. I'm such a horrible daughter to ask my parents to send me here then throw it down the drain with my crappy attitude.

Something weird about being here is that the more I'm away from my ED, the greater the desires get. Also, I really don't remember how bad I felt and how completely horrific my life was 2 weeks ago, and for the past few years. So not remembering the past makes it seem not as bad. I'm afraid that it will take a serious relapse when I go home to feel the pain and hate my ED enough to not go back to it.

Random thoughts...

There are girls that are refusing their Boost. The fact that I can even do it shows strength. Not trying to compare. But I do have something. Amy told me last night that I have so much passion, I need to channel it into the right things.

- Right now, I'm trying not to worry about eating in general; all I really need to do is focus on one meal at a time.
- I wish I could relax. I'm so anxious, especially in the morning, it's nuts! I'm trying techniques, imagery, focusing on senses, etc. but nothing seems to help. God, please help me to calm down and find something to help me relax.

Having suicidal thoughts scared me because they were definitely a first. I couldn't really explain my situation on that Thursday night until I thought of the Titanic analogy. There's the scene where Rose is hanging off the back of the ship, about to jump, then Jack comes and talks her through it. Later he says, "You wouldn't have jumped." And Rose replies, "How do you know...who are you to tell me what I will and won't do?" And he goes, "You would have done it already." Then also she says how she wanted a way out. That is exactly how I felt and still feel, to an extent. In the midst of panic and anger and hopeless misery, I hysterically went searching for a solution. I wanted out. I would have jumped by now and I didn't. But that feeling of hopelessness is so unbearable.

July 16, 2006
It's so amazing to me still that I can eat all this food and not gain a tremendous amount of weight! It's scary and I can't imagine eating that much in the real world, but it's what I need to do here. At first it was really hard and it still is but every day it gets a little bit easier. One meal at a time Sharon!

July 17, 2006
I am thinking of recovery as if I get one thing out of it; eating healthier, accepting my body, etc. then it is an accomplishment. Thinking of how much I have to change: exercising less, not restricting, not purging, not binging, not tearing myself down, etc. makes this too overwhelming. It's not that I don't want to fully recover, it's that I find it too

depressing and stressful to right now. I've tried to eliminate stress here, but actually I feel a lot worse.

Jason shared this quote today in Chapel. He is so kind and constantly reminds us that we are princesses, valued greatly by God, and that he prays for us to see ourselves that way. I have so much strength and potential through God. I need to pray that he will help me to believe it.

"Our deepest fear is not that we are inadequate. Our deepest fear is that we are powered beyond measure. It is our light, not our darkness, that most frightens us. We ask ourselves, who am I to be brilliant, gorgeous, talented and fabulous? Actually, who are you not to be? You are a child of God. Your playing small doesn't serve the world. There is nothing enlightened about shrinking so that other people won't feel insecure around you." -Nelson Mandela

July 21, 2006
9:55 p.m.

Wow, I seriously can't believe that I've been here 3 weeks! It seriously has gone by fast and I am proud of myself for sticking it out. Since my friend Ashley has been here, things have been going so much better. I found the perfect friend to open up to and relate to. We have so much fun together, and encourage each other to keep going. It's truly a blessing! I still have 24 days left, and am honestly excited about what will happen. I think that after my family week, it will start to fly by even more.

Today I ate:
Breakfast: yogurt parfait, banana, coffee
Snack: fruit snacks, Boost
Lunch: apple, chips, tuna fish sandwich
Snack: yogurt raisins, pudding, Boost

Dinner: turkey burger, fruit salad
Snack-trail mix

It is so foreign to me that I am eating all that when before I was eating that amount all week, or probably less. I know I have gained weight, even though just yesterday "Heather" told me she looks at me and feels bad about herself because I'm a "smaller" girl. Even though I don't see myself that way at all. I feel so fat. I'm actually getting hungry more though, which is scary. I don't want to eat anymore because then I feel like I'll gain more. I can't honestly say that I'll keep the weight on when I return home. I think I'll try to lose it in a healthy way. At least I'll be able to exercise more, and not have to eat until I'm uncomfortably full, or force myself to eat food I hate. So I'm not sure how I'll write my commitment letter. I guess I can just be honest about what I am for sure committing to. Which is not purging, having accountability, expressing my feelings, and seeing my support team. Or I can just not write one. Hmmm I can't honestly say that I will stick to my exercise plan. I will probably do more each day. But I am not here for total recovery. I'm here to learn how to be healthy and control my weight in a healthy way and learn how to express my feelings and deal with feelings in better coping ways. Tonight a bunch of girls and I snuck down to the pool. ☺ Fun stuff.

July 23, 2006

I'm halfway done! I'm so excited. I don't get how people don't want to leave. I mean I know I'll be sad probably to leave the friends I've made but I will definitely want to go home. I'm glad I only have 3 weeks left. I never thought I would make it but I know I will now. One more week until family week. That will be exciting, yet hard. I can't wait to see people who love me and know me better than anyone here. I think today is my last Boost. I'm glad that I won't be intentionally gaining weight anymore. I am really depressed because of my body. I just obsess about how fat I am and how I'll get back to where I was. Or at least half way there. I think it's so mean to ask people to give up 3 or4 addictions—restricting, binging, purging, over exercising, etc. when I think if I can leave here and not throw up, it will be a miracle. I feel like it's a fucking waste of time. 22 days of trying this, and I'm secretly so excited to lose weight when I get out of here, but I won't tell anyone that. I feel that I will get something out of this treatment, but it won't be my last time.

July 25, 2006

I only have 20 days left! I really can't believe it's almost time to go. I'm excited to go home and get back to my normal life. I'm getting to know the girls better and enjoying the time with them. It makes the days go faster. I realized today from giving my life story that I minimize my problems a lot. I don't want to admit I think things are a big deal because I feel like everyone will say they're not. But if it is a big deal to me, I need to accept that and admit it.

Thursday I have restaurant challenge. My goal is to eat a cheeseburger and fries, not because I want it, but because I have to have disgusting fried food. Then perhaps ice cream… not sure about that. But I want to prove to myself that I can do it. Conquering fear foods gives me power. I am also going to start looking at the snack options right before snack and eventually just going up and choosing what I want, rather than planning it out all day.

July 27, 2006 –Day 27 Thank God!

I am so overwhelmed right now with recovery. I feel like a failure. I wish I had the drive and strength that other girls have, like Caitlin. Even looking at some of the girls with feeding tubes makes me feel awful about myself. I'm such a failure; I can't even have a severe enough ED to get a tube. I'm pissed off at Katie. She said my body fat was 1% higher than when I came in, and it wasn't ever low, it was in the normal range. Which makes me pissed off for having to gain weight. She just wanted me to get fat, with no good reason because I feel soooo unbelievably worse about my body. I don't care how little weight it is to everyone else—I notice so much. Body image therapy one-on-one today didn't even help today. I hated "Shannon," the body image and art therapist because she is so fake and I can't talk to her. Estimating my measurements made me sick because I still hated how big they were and knew it would have been smaller before I came here. I am going to lose the weight I've gained.

I'm afraid to go home and go see Victoria and everything. I hate myself for not letting this place help me the way it could have. I'm trying but I honestly feel nothing helps. I am going to feel like more of a failure when I go home and everyone thinks I'm no better. I just don't think anyone believes me that I want recovery. But who would want to live like this?

I hate the fact I can't talk to Sara. I could, but I know she'll probably talk to Katie, and they'll think I'm backsliding. Maybe it's all a show. I'm playing the game and gaining the weight because I have to, not because it's my choice. I hate it,

I hate it, I hate it! I hate myself! I don't know why or how to stop or why I do or if I'll ever feel better.

July 29, 2006

 I'm trying to listen to my body and eat what I'm hungry for, but I still am cutting back on my EQ's and meals. I can leave 2-3 bites at lunch and dinner so I usually always leave some just so I don't have to finish it. Now I can have 4-8 EQ's and I don't really care what Katie says or thinks, I'm not going to push myself to eat more even if I'm hungry. I am hungry a lot now, sometimes all day, but I love it because I haven't felt it in awhile. I've been so full, which makes me feel disgusting, wanting to do ED behaviors, and lose weight. At least if I weighed less I wouldn't hate myself. Anyways, yesterday I had 6 EQ's; I did awful and couldn't control myself at nighttime snack. But today I'll only have 5, and maybe 5 again tomorrow and Sunday, and 4 after that. I don't want to eat too much but I need to eat enough. I think I am okay, I just still have some thoughts that people think are critical barriers in my recovery, but what the hell—they don't know me!

 I really want help when I get home and I'm so scared of disappointing them. But I'm so incredibly sick of therapy. I hate sitting in class after class, I get sooo bored and can't concentrate. I am getting less anxiety but I feel ADHD and my dyslexia is getting worse which makes me scared that I will never do well in school again and like an even BIGGER failure.

 I do need to work on liking myself. Sara says I need to "be nicer to myself." And we decided that even if I don't accept my body, at least I could like myself. I will keep trying.

 I'm so tired of going to all these classes. I know I sit in school all day but that is something that I'm really interested in and want to learn about. Of course I like the nutrition classes here, but all the stupid skills classes and stuff just piss me off. I hate being treated like a little kid, having to do assignments. It's like I wish I would put more effort in and give things a chance but I don't. Well, I do. I have tried everything I've been told to, but I don't like doing things because someone tells me, or I'm doing it for someone else. And I know what works for me. I'm glad that I finally told Sara how I felt. She said it well today when she said, "I think we connect well as people, but in therapy, we aren't communicating well." Which is probably just all my fault. I really liked the equine experiential and I hope I can do it again. I like the restaurant challenge, cardio class, art therapy, ropes course, equine, etc. because then I can do stuff and learn from the experience, which is how I learn. It's not that I don't like therapy with Sara one-on-one, but I like groups better, and I feel bad for getting so mad at her. I wish I could open up more. Once again I push people away who try to help. I don't get how I feel. I wish I could finally be committed to recovery 100% but I'm still not. I feel like I need to get worse again and get help on my own and do what works for me. I know I asked my parents to come here because I thought it would be the help I need. I guess I just need to get what I can out of this, and trust that God will show me. I feel so much pressure because my parents did pay so much money for me to come. I feel pressure that improving one thing isn't enough, it has to be 50 things. It makes me physically sick to think about how this is turning out. I know that it's probably my fault, but I can't just take away this unbelievable guilt. I can't take the pressure.

I feel like I'm in this perfect bubble world, unable to

do ED behaviors and like I'm just playing the game but so not even able to realize how bad I was when I was home. It's almost too easy here. I'm doing it "perfectly" by eating, not exercising, not purging, not even really comparing myself to other girl's bodies. I hate being looked at as having it all together or whatever. I try to emphasize how much I'm struggling to my peers and Sara. But for some reason I can't. I feel disconnected from myself again. I don't know if I'm pushing my emotions aside and not letting myself feel, even when I sit with them.

Equine Experiential #1

"Temptation Alley"

I loved my experience earlier today yet it was so frustrating. At first I wasn't that afraid, even having to ride bareback. But the task didn't seem that difficult, like I thought when I first started recovery. I thought that it would be easy. There were 2 ropes coming off of the bridal that Sara and the other woman were holding. At the end, the alley was a mess, like my life...out of control and falling apart. I began this task knowing 2 rules: that I couldn't let the horse, Sam eat the food (temptation), couldn't allow the equine lady and Sara (my support) in my boundaries and I couldn't step out. Breaking those rules caused me to have a consequence, which I chose, which was to stop for 10 seconds. So at first I thought I couldn't ask for help, couldn't use the lead ropes myself, couldn't control the horse, etc.

Riding on Sam represented my life, and me, but I specifically labeled Sam as my ED. Each temptation that came in the way was a chance for me to take control or give into the temptations of restricting, not following my meal *plan, purging, weighing myself, over exercising, and binging and purging.*

I realized I had to ask for help, to hold the ropes, and ask my support to walk beside me and help me. It was frustrating because I wanted a specific answer on how to do it successfully. I had the drive and willpower as I do in recovery, to conquer the task. But I felt like a failure because I couldn't do it. I kept kicking Sam, telling him to go, and pulling hard to stop. I know I confused him and gave him mixed messages. I should have been more confident and stern but I really didn't know what horse skills to use.

This journey was so like my recovery. I have tried so many times and screwed up.

July 31, 2006

I'm about to leave for family week. I'm excited and happy to see what my parents will learn. They need to learn so much. I was surprised yesterday that I almost wanted to go to the step-down program, Remuda Life. But I really don't think that is the best thing, I would get home a day before school starts and that would be too crazy for me. I really want to go home. Well, 14 days left at least. I am just going to focus on getting through it.

Scarily enough, I have had temptations to self-harm. I don't know if it's just being around people who do it, or learning about a new idea. My roommate hurt herself a few nights ago in our room. She used a belt buckle and cut her wrist. I almost was amazed that she actually got around the rules and managed to still do it even though they think they have so much control over us. But I'm also scared that I might try self-harm if I give up my eating disorder. I don't

think I would but it still scares me. Why do I keep getting interested in the craziest, unhealthy things?
Day 39

August 6, 2006

It's my last week here at Remuda. I have so many mixed emotions, but my biggest are probably frustration, anxiety, and motivation. I'm frustrated at Sara, her way of trying to talk me into the Remuda Life program, which is not realistic for me at this point in my life. I am mad at myself for not being nicer to her, and not maybe getting quite as much out of our sessions as I could have. I feel like she just kept making me do worksheets or "stuff" when all I wanted and needed was to talk about how I really was feeling. I don't feel like she listens or understands me even though she says she is "on my side." I like her and I think we would be good friends but for some reason I don't click well with her, and haven't been able to open up to her.

I'm anxious and irritable after spending this long in a house with 15 girls. I'm about to snap. I don't know if I can take some of them much longer. AHHH!!! Oh well. I'll be leaving in 6 days! ☺ I think part of my depression today is because of having family week last week, being busy and everything, then having to sit around here all day, bored and alone, and no desire to talk to anyone here. I'm anxious to go home, I can't wait! It'll be such a challenge and I'm ready to face it and overcome this.

I'm becoming so bored here, because it's too easy now. I can eat my meals already prepared, portioned, and handed to me regularly. I can go to the classes and listen, talk and learn and it's great, but in reality, I'm not going to live in an eating disorder recovery bubble world forever. It's so easy for *me, the other girls are more triggered over things that don't bother me, or things I never even notice. That's a good thing because it means food is not a big deal anymore to me. Not that it won't be hard at home—I know it will be. But I can't wait to get out of the comfort here and deal with the struggles I'll have in the real world.*

Going out with my parents on pass this weekend was great. It was challenging but I felt I did good eating what I truly wanted, in a correct portion, and being able to enjoy it. I don't remember feeling guilty after eating. I didn't have a desire to purge. Shopping with my mom was fun! I bought clothes I liked and looked good in. I still hate my body but I'll work on that. I want recovery so bad but I want to lose weight MUCH more than before. I'm so unbelievably pissed. I hate it here. I'm sick of pressure that everyone puts on me. I want to be encouraged for the good decisions I make. Everyone just seems to put greater expectations on me than I can handle. I can't take the pressure to do more when I'm already overwhelmed with my commitments I don't know if I can handle. I feel like a failure because I'm not doing what everyone else wants. I hate myself.

Day 40—5 more days!

August 8, 2006

Equine Experiential #2!!!

So I had my 2nd one-on-one equine and it was so eye-opening! This time, I was with the horse Bella inside the ring. My task was to get her over the obstacle, and the only rules were that I couldn't touch the horse, and couldn't bride her with food. But I could use anything in the pen.

So first I took down the pole off the 2 blocks and put in on the ground in order to make it easier on myself. Then

I asked for help, and the answer was that horses respond to pressure, but I didn't understand how I could apply that if I couldn't touch Bella. Oh yeah, also, I labeled Bella as me, I was my mind (conscious), the pole was my eating disorder, and going over it would be recovery. The equine ladies were was my treatment team and family and friends, and Sara was God. I realized I need to have God be a bigger part in my recovery. I haven't been praying or asking for him to help me. I wish I could, I just don't have the desire. And I hate myself for it. After putting the pole on the ground, I kind of tried to approach Bella to make her step over it but she freaked out and kept running around. I didn't understand how to apply pressure when I couldn't touch her. I quit trying because I give up easily when I have no clue what to do next. I was mad at my support for not helping me more. They couldn't give me the answer, of course, but they could help, and did, but I didn't listen. Sara had to be hard on me and tell me that for most of my stay here I had not taken the advice or help given to me, and I gave up trying when I didn't have a set answer. But then she said that when I have used what I've been given, I was able to make progress.

I didn't see how a stupid horse was going to help me in recovery. I was still pissed off and frustrated and started crying! I'm amazed I actually got to that point. Finally Sara picked up a stick and I asked her to wave it at Bella. She was cornered with her head hanging over the fence. So I moved the pole behind her and placed my support around as barriers. Then also put the obstacles to block her in. And lo and behold—it worked! I was shocked yet thrilled I actually did it. I didn't want to fail at another task. I did use the advice that was given to me and had a lot of help from "God" but he helped me figure it out myself.

So I kept crying...I learned that I will face obstacles every day in recovery. And I need to make the decision to overcome them even when they seem impossible. I can use my support team, God, and friends for help but eventually I have to make the ultimate choice.
Day 41

August 10, 2006
I hate my life. It's official. I hate what I've done and where I've gotten myself. I don't know if I hate my eating disorder, though. I hate Sharon with an eating disorder. But I also hate Sharon without one, too. I feel like my life is worthless. I feel so guilty for my parents having to pay for this. I feel like I wasted their money. How could I not feel this way?!? I feel like I have wasted all these day here...at least most of them. I see the new girls talking about how committed they are to each day and everything in this program, while I feel like I haven't given it my all and I HATE that. I didn't come in thinking, "Wow, I'm gonna do this! I CAN do it." I thought more like, "Oh well, I'm here, I guess I'll try. Who cares if I recover or not...it's my life." I know I HAVE made progress and family week was amazing and I am committed to recovery, but I haven't done it with the ambition I would have hoped. The story of my life is going somewhere, doing something, and wasting time. I'm such an unbelievably worthless human being!!!! I suck at everything and my decisions never please anybody, not even me.
I am so incredibly worried about home and not having a job. I feel like a loser for quitting it before I came. Why couldn't I have just been honest, took a time of leave, and came back so at least I'd HAVE a job and not stress about

the money until I can find a new job. God, I hate it. Why can't I ever be satisfied and do the right things? I hate it that I still don't have a better relationship with you, God. I wasted time here. I haven't asked you to be a part of my recovery. I'm still angry with you and I don't know why. I need someone to help me with my issues beyond the eating disorder:

> *Perfectionism*
> *Self-hate*
> *Guilt*
> *Self-punishment*
> *Worthlessness*
> *Anger*
> *Depression*

I pray that my fill-in counselor will be good for me until Victoria gets back. I just want so badly to talk to her again. Maybe now that I have a different outlook and that I want to make the most of it I will do better at dealing with deeper things.

Isaiah 43:18-19 "Forget the former things; do not dwell on the past. See, I am doing a new thing! Now it spring up; do you not perceive it? I am making a way in the desert, and streams in the wasteland."

August 12, 2006

I'm pissed at life. At my family. At Sara. At myself. At this fucking eating disorder and at Satan for making it so appealing and convincing me I don't want to stop.

I just want to move into my apartment. I just want to be on my own. Why pay $300 a month for an apartment I'm not going to live in?!? It's a waste. And I'm not going to live in a controlled home again. I'm just not. I'm an adult and *this is my recovery. I can't take the pressure from everyone and the guilt for not doing exactly what they want.*

I WILL lose the weight I gained here because I HATE my body 1000 times more now and look and feel DISGUSTING! I'm going to maintain a lower weight. Weighing what I do now makes me restrict, and want to purge more! I'll accept my weight when I'm ready to. I know I have to recover. I can't go on with an eating disorder, but it has to be when Sharon is ready, and taking the steps I am willing to take.

CHAPTER 10

Somehow I left Remuda with a good plan in place, and actually some motivation that I was going to conquer this. My friends, therapist, and the workers there were encouraging. I was glad that they seemed to have some faith in me, and could see a change in me during my stay there. My commitments that I did end up making were that I would see my doctor, a dietician, find a support group and continue counseling in some way, until Victoria returned. I also wanted to try an outpatient program that was three times a week. I came home with an intense fear, but I was determined to try to eat on my own and follow my meal plan as best as I could. As I looked in the refrigerator for something to eat for breakfast, it was foreign because I hadn't even done that for a month and half. I was frustrated at myself for still not being sure I wanted to recover, even after all that had happened that summer.

I did find a support group which I tried, saw my

doctor, made an appointment with a dietician, and went to counseling once at Kent State, and once with Victoria's fill-in. I didn't feel as if I could talk to her. She came across as really sympathetic and I got the vibe that she felt bad for me. I couldn't take that and wasn't motivated to give it another shot. She kept saying how well I was doing and how I should be proud of myself, but I wasn't. I hated myself. All I could see was my failure. I didn't want to open up and kept my thoughts to myself. I also went to the outpatient program, because I figured I should give it a try, but I was basically just going to please my family, once again. It wasn't what I thought it would be. The skills we learned for an hour were exactly the same and I had *just* learned at Remuda, one hour was eating dinner—which I was doing all right on my own, and the last hour was a support group, which I already had found. I realized that this wasn't the help I needed, because there were no dieticians there or individual counseling. I was preparing the next day for the hour drive there, when I realized—I didn't have to go to please everyone because it wasn't their treatment. I had to do what was best for me. And I finally had the courage to do so.

After two weeks of very little therapy, yet still eating well and not purging, I moved into my apartment near Kent State, started a new job at a café, and went back to college full-time all within two days. I was always able to handle so much stress before, I was certain I could deal with all these changes. I didn't know what to do, so I put on the biggest mask I have ever worn in my life. I began purging again before I moved into my apartment, immediately began restricting, and working out constantly. And even worse, I added cutting as a way to cope and taking laxatives for the first time. I felt more and more worthless and hopeless every day.

I had the mindset that when I got home from treatment, I not only would not struggle again, but *I should not* struggle. My expectations for myself were higher than anyone's. I couldn't bring myself to admit to anyone that my eating disorder was worse than before I ever had treatment. I had put so much pressure on myself to succeed at this, when I made the first compromise, it led me into completely giving up, and believing that I was doomed to fail and never recover.

After being home for almost a month, starving all day, and binging and purging whenever I could get away with it, I was too overwhelmed with school, work, and trying to live on my own again to keep going. I purged approximately 50 times one day, and was so appalled at the inability to control myself that I decided that the only answer to end my pain was to end my life. On Friday, September 8th, I decided to take 2 boxes of laxatives. I wanted to punish myself for my failure, for what a horrible person I was, and to rid my body of any remaining disgusting food I had put in it. I was disappointed that other than being sick all night, there were no other effects. I developed a plan the next morning and was determined to follow through on it, and end this agony once and for all. I thought I wanted to die at the time, but I realize looking back that what I really wanted was to show everyone how much pain I was in. I was just too ashamed to say it. I *was* indifferent whether or not I would wake up the next day. But I knew if I hurt myself at least I wouldn't have to get up and live the next day, and finally everyone might understand I needed more help.

So, without thinking, I went and bought three boxes of laxatives, hoping this might do a little more damage, and I threw in a bottle of 150 Advil just for kicks. I figured that would be enough of an overdose to knock me out and kill me in my sleep. I went home and binged and purged, just trying to get rid of the overwhelming emotions I was feeling, and crying the whole time. I was so sick of living like this, and wanted out. I was determined to finally go through with my plan. I took the pills. 3 or 4 at a time. As quickly as I could. I screamed out to God, asking him why, if he loved me, he was letting me do this to myself. I couldn't control myself, I couldn't stop. After the pills were gone, I cut my wrists, knowing it wouldn't kill me but hoping I would lose some blood, and punishing myself with pain for being such an awful person. After realizing I wasn't dying immediately, I became scared. I thought, "Maybe I don't want to die." So, I went to the bathroom and made myself throw up one time, just to see if maybe I could eliminate some of the toxins in my body. I believe I eliminated just enough. And then I did what only someone who desperately wanted to live would do. I called my friend "Laci." I told her what I did. And I asked her for help.

Laci was probably the best friend to deal with me at the time, because she did not panic whatsoever (at least she didn't show it!). She came over and drove around a little, because she didn't know the nearest hospital, and finally called 911. They told her to go to the fire station in Kent. I felt stupid. That's the only word I can use to describe how I felt at the time. I had failed at recovery from my eating disorder, and now had failed at trying to kill myself. The paramedics didn't really help my feelings, either.

It began with a guy asking me my major. I replied, "health education." Of course I got the usual, "Oh you're in *health* when you have an eating disorder?" Yes, thanks for pointing that out. I wasn't aware of the irony.

"Don't you know Advil doesn't even kill you right away?" No, obviously not, or we wouldn't be having this conversation would we?

"It will kill you in a year when you have liver failure." Thank you, just made my night better.

"Why did you cut your wrists? That doesn't even solve anything." Do you really think I'm been thinking clearly tonight? Way to make a suicidal girl feel even worse.

Then he taped my IV right over the open cut. That made me happy. "Hmmm that's gonna suck when I pull that off tomorrow," I thought. And then I just decided to tune this dude out.

Luckily when I arrived at the hospital, I was taken care of by the nicest people in the world who actually talked to me like I *had* a brain. I drank some charcoal, to absorb the poison in my body. It was disgusting but I imagined the worst was over. A couple of hours later, when I finally got to my room, I realized I was going to puke (and not intentionally for once). It turned out, puking charcoal is worse than drinking it. Black charcoal came up constantly all night, as well as the 75 laxatives doing their job. I would lie down for 15 minutes and be up again, over the toilet, trying to figure out which I'd

came out in almost every piece I made. It also gradually became a form of worship for me, as I would pray and incorporate Scripture into my art. I actually *felt* again. Some of my art was done with extreme emotion and an expression of my fear in recovery, hatred of myself, or love and hope I had in Christ. This newfound talent also gave me the ambition of becoming a counselor and art therapist, which I actively began pursuing.

The next couple of months were full of ups and downs. Days of commitments to recovery, and days I was set on throwing in the towel. But the most important thing I learned through this time was that I made it. I got through the urges and the thoughts that were so overwhelming, sometimes in positive ways, and other times in negative ways. However, I didn't give up. And the fact that I had enough strength to keep going even in my darkest days, gave me hope that I *would* make it. That God *would* bring me through.

*   *   *   *

August 28, 2006

I'm going to be honest. I relapsed. Not just for an hour, or a day…a weekend, and today. Why did it start? I don't know exactly. But I do know that I dealt with my feelings in the most unhealthy, painful, easiest ways. As I read through my progression of thoughts leading up to what I did, it makes sense. I ate more than usual (on Saturday), ate a snack out of boredom, and then felt I had to punish myself for not listening to my body.

-Then I threw up, to punish myself

-I felt guilty for purging, breaking my promise not to purge again and failing (in my mind)

-I binged because I figured, "Screw it! I already failed today...why try?"

-I purged excessively because I wanted to feel pain, get relief, and from fear of gaining weight.

-Didn't want recovery—I was HOPELESS

-Hated myself even after I ate a healthy dinner

-Cut my wrist with a razor for purging earlier

-Also because I felt I was wrong for feeling hopeless and not wanting recovery. I feel like I shouldn't have those thoughts after being at Remuda.

-I felt pain, saw blood, and got relief

-I then punished myself by not letting myself sleep.

-I stayed up till 5 a.m., ruminating in my thoughts, reliving the behaviors I had done that day.

-I knew I needed God—and I cried out to him. I felt alone and like I could talk to no one.

-I feel so much shame still—I'm supposed to be getting <u>better</u> and all I feel is like I'm just adding another harmful behavior and that is a failure. I hate myself for it. ☹

Sunday I was tired from not sleeping. I binged again... for the purpose of purging. I didn't eat that much but I just wanted a release from the INTENSE pain that I was feeling. My thoughts and urges have never been so strong as the night before. I had no one to talk to. If I did tell Amy or my parents about the self-harm they would flip. I can't do it to them. They're already beyond worried.

I feel guilty for doing it, for feeling so much pain, self-hate, and depression. Why? Why do I feel this way?!? I don't want to. I don't think I want to. I want it to go away.

Maybe I'm not talking about my feelings enough and it's coming out as aggressive acts on my body.

I left Josh and Amy's a complete mess. I was so sad and disappointed in myself for purging everything and the cutting I had done there. And the disappointment and burden I felt that I was to them.

Today—no better. I ate breakfast. Then was starving around 3:00. I had a ton of food, purged, and chugged some Gatorade to fix my electrolytes. Then I went to work out for 45 minutes.

September 1, 2006

I'm not motivated to do anything. Nothing. I hate getting up every day because I don't feel like living. I hate that I feel this way. I thought being at home would be better. I guess I was wrong. One day I know I will be happy, it's just the process that sucks. I have such an intense pain that I don't even know where it comes from. But I do know what releases it (temporarily anyway)—purging, starving, exercising…and now cutting. I'm glad that I told Amy. I had to tell someone. I haven't done it for a week, and don't really want to, which is good. I asked Josh if he thought I was screwed up and he said he hoped not. I'm pretty sure I am.

September 2, 2006

I failed today. Or I took 500 steps back—one of the two. I hate the fact that I ate so much, and purged soooo much, not even trying to use my brain or the skills I learned, or even the people and resources right before me. Today my binging consisted of like 3000 calories. Anyways—I feel so stupid. I hate it, I feel so sick. Amy almost caught me at her house…I'm sure she knew what I was doing but she didn't say anything. I'm on my period and hate that because it means I have enough body fat to have a period. That means I am fat, so of course I want to punish my body. I have the worst cramps of my life, and I won't take anything for it. I'm in a lot of pain, but I feel like I deserve it. I love to feel pain—it distracts me from my real issues. At least for a little while. I can forget about my self-hatred if I'm thinking about how bad my body hurts at the moment. What can I say—I am screwed up! I can somewhat see the mental chaos going on because with the eating disorder, at least it made me skinny. Not happy, but I got something "good" out of it. I lost weight by starving and purging and over exercising. It does work. Exercising does make your body look better. Cutting just doesn't. I don't get it because it doesn't give me anything except a scar. Well, relief—but the purging gives me that too. Nothing to show for physically, though. I don't get it. I'm alone, and scared. I don't feel like I can tell any of my friends (except Laci), and Amy I guess. But I feel so bad going to her. She already has so much stress and worries about me not knowing a lot. I don't have anyone to really call at <u>any</u> time. I did call Lane yesterday and she was watching a movie and said she would call me today. I felt so alone and awful. I called her, and Kelly, and Laci. No one was there for me. I guess that's how humans are—they are bound to let me down. Maybe I just expect too much out of people.

September 3, 2006

I basically binged and purged for the last 24 hours, other than the few hours I slept. I feel OUT OF CONTROL!!! I *didn't want to do what I did to the extreme but I felt like I had to. I purged the Chex mix and M&M's I had last night, and then woke up this morning craving to do it again and again. I'm such a failure. I hate myself. Oh yeah—last night I cut myself more after purging I just lost it in the bathroom and grabbed the razor without even thinking. I absolutely am DISGUSTED in myself. I'm not supposed to be doing this. I'm in recovery and shouldn't be making this big of a mistake. I'm so numb; I don't really feel anything anymore (which is nice, yet scary to me). I want to feel bad about it so I won't do it again. The scariest thing is that I seriously couldn't stop throwing up. I just kept eating and kept purging. Every time I felt dehydrated and hungry—I felt that I needed something healthy to keep down. That's why I'd eat crackers and the veggie wrap, and the yogurt. But even the fact that I ate something healthy was more than I could handle. I hate food so much because I feel gross when I eat and have to get rid of it. After failing every time at that, I tried to drink Gatorade to rehydrate myself. I couldn't keep that down, either. Then finally I had Diet Coke (0 calories…) but I still felt full, and therefore FAT in my mind. Then I just decided to drink a bunch of water and coffee, and purged that too. Why can't I even keep liquids down?!?! My body needs fluids! And nutrients. I know this! Why don't I care about myself???? I don't know what to do.*

September 6, 2006

    Yesterday I binged and purged but not quite as much as the "24 hour" binge/purge I went on before. I just ate a few random things, and I did exercise but I didn't cut. ☺ *I made the decision today—I am not going to self-harm!*

God, please help me! I know I can only overcome this with your strength. But that's the truth—I CAN overcome it!

I know I can also overcome the eating disorder, but it's so hard when I don't even have the desire sometimes (like today). I'm trying to think of strategies I used in Remuda when I was having a hard time. I have a few:

*Being honest—saying "I don't want to recover" or "I just want to go home," or "This sucks," etc.

*Telling someone how I feel, just talking to anyone

*Telling myself I could eat again tomorrow (if I have an urge to binge/purge at night)

*Positive self-talk at meals

*Recognizing the good I had accomplished

*Reminding myself how good it felt to be healthy (not feeling like I'm going to pass out all the time)

I actually threw up in my car today in a cup. Then at the rec, in the bathroom upstairs that no one ever uses. I can seriously just throw up without even sticking my fingers down my throat! I just have to lean over. Kinda cool. Kinda gross.

I am just waiting for the day to come when I wake up and feel gung-ho about recovery. I guess it's not going to happen quite like that. I have to make the right decision every day... it's eventually just up to me in the end. I firmly believe that. And I can do it with the Lord's help. Today the last thing I wanted to do was eat the burrito. But I did! And I kept that down at least.

I talked to Lane tonight. She seems to understand more than anyone else. I love her! ☺ What a great friend. Tomorrow I have Kent counseling and shall call the dietician.

*   *   *   *

September 12, 2006
God,

For the first time in months, I can sit and be at peace. I'm not hopeless, and I'm not worried about tomorrow. My despair, agony, fear, depression, and hopelessness are being replaced by your love, your comfort, your joy, and by your secure arms around me, holding me close to you. It has been such a long time since I have known any of these things. You brought me through a great valley—so very low and long and hard. I got lost along the journey again and again. If only I could have looked up to see you were right there with me the entire time. I know this is so true, and all I can say is that you are wonderful! I can't dwell on the past and worry about what I didn't see then. I see you everywhere now. You never have left me because you love me so much. Even at my very lowest—when all I thought I could hear was the devil's voice telling me to hurt myself—I know you were there— fighting for me because I couldn't do it alone. Thank you for holding on to me, for loving me so much even when at times I didn't accept your love. Thank you for your mighty power. You defeated evil. You won, God! Thank you for life, for a new day, for a new start. I know you have amazing things for me, and it will begin with healing. I will let you in God, I so desperately need you. Amen.

September 14, 2006
God,

I keep having bad thoughts again. I don't want to. I hate feeling this way. I want to die. Take them away. Please take them away. I want to drive a knife into my arm. I'm being attacked. Tell Satan to go away—to leave me alone. I can't fight it but YOU can! Please help me, please give me peace. Be with me, hold me, and draw me close to you. I felt so good the past few days—I thought that this was over. But I know it's not that easy. It will take a lot of time.

Psalm 91:14-15 "Because [Sharon] loves me," says the Lord, "I will rescue her, I will protect her, for she acknowledges my name. She will call upon me, and I will answer her; I will be with her in trouble, I will deliver and honor her."

Thank you for providing that scripture for me, God. I know you are there. Please rescue me. I have so many confusing thoughts racing through my mind now...I'm overwhelmed and don't know even what to pray. You can hear my cry though, and know exactly what I need. I want to overcome this so badly! You will give me victory! I know it. You are so faithful. You always have been so good to me. I love you.

"You give it all up, or you keep it all." –friend from Remuda

September 16, 2006
God,

I feel so much pain right now. I hate my life—I'm so anxious about money, and what to do with my life. I'm hurt that I have hurt people around me. I hate myself for the mistakes I've made. Why can't I have the grace to forgive myself? Please help me to forgive myself, Amy, my parents, friends, whoever—for doing or saying the wrong things. I know I'm not perfect and neither are they. May forgiveness be extended both ways in whatever circumstances necessary. I want to be on good terms with my support system.

I still want to die though. I don't have motivation to

live. I want to starve myself. I feel so fat. I just want to starve until I die. I feel so selfish—like I ruin people's lives—and it would just be easier if I weren't around. But I guess that is selfish, because then that would hurt them and make their lives harder, too. I need you…I at least feel I can be honest and I have a desire to be close to you.

September 18, 2006
5:45 a.m.
God—

I just drank Gatorade and want to purge. I feel so disgusting. Why do I crave it so much?!?! I wish it wasn't so appealing. I still feel like I'll never overcome this. I keep picturing myself going back to how I was last fall. I ask that you would take these thoughts away. Please intervene and invade my mind, my doubts, and my desires. Turn them from the evil desires I currently have to a desire to follow you, and fall in love with you. I can't sleep…please settle my mind. Help me to feel better. Do a mighty work tomorrow. Amen.

Exodus 14:14 "The Lord will fight for you; you need only to be still."

Bulimanacompulsivorexia -(n)- when you have no idea what eating disorder you have and don't fit into a doctor's mold. Screw the DSM! ☺   —created by a fellow patient at Remuda

September 20, 2006
3:17 a.m.

I am running down a long dark tunnel.
I'm running fast, alone

Running aimlessly, trying to find the end.
I don't know how I got here,
Trapped in this darkness.
I feel like a horrible person,
Life didn't used to be like this.
A thought runs through my mind
"You're worthless."
I push it aside.
I'm determined to get out on my own.
There's no one to ask,
And if there was, what could they say?
I got myself here in the first place.
I deserve to struggle until I get out.
If I ever do get out.
I want to quit, but a voice in my head screams advice.
"Food is bad! Eating is for weak people!"
"Don't eat today—eating only makes you fat!"
"Purge that, you don't need food!"
It makes sense to me.
I try it.
I like it.
At least for a while.
It calms me, it brings relief.
It makes me feel in control.
I'm still trapped.
I don't think I'll get out
But I don't need to.
I'm fine with my friend.
The voice is louder and more intense.
It comes more often.
Soon it's all I think about.
After days and days and days,

This is not enough.
I'm still lost, alone, and scared.
I'm not happy anymore, I can't even fake it.
I hear it again.
"Take these, you'll lose weight."
Okay, I agree.
Whatever to make me happy.
It's not enough.
"You're never gonna be free, just give up!"
"No one cares about you—look what you've done to yourself."
"There's no hope for you!"
I believe it.
"Take more, take more, take more!!!!"
I can't stop.
"Cut yourself—you deserve the pain!!!"
I am. I'm bleeding.
"DIE!!"
I look up…I can see the end of the tunnel.
It's not a light, it's the world.
Someone takes my hand
And leads me out.
I'm finally free,
I'm finally safe.
I hear a new voice, it whispers softly.
I walk.
I'm with my Savior.
He uncovers the lies
He unmasks his truth.
I'm not worthless.
I can finally begin to believe it
As I begin a new life.

September 21, 2006
God,

All I want to do right now is purge. I have so many emotions…anger, disappointment, regret, hopelessness, disgust, and sadness. Anger at Victoria, for wanting my parents to come back to counseling. Anger at my parents for being willing to help but wanting to fix me. I just feel like I get so upset over nothing. They do so much for me and have shown me such love through everything.

I'm disappointed in myself. I skipped group tonight. I just didn't want to go at all. I wanted to binge and purge, or just throw away my chicken wrap. I came back to my apartment and cried, and decided to eat it. I cried the whole time; I didn't want it at all. I almost started to gag. It made me feel sick, I didn't want to eat so much. I wish I <u>wanted</u> recovery more. I just want to say— "Screw recovery!" at times like this. I don't feel like I'll ever recover. Please reassure me it's possible.

You gave me victory tonight! Thank you. I know it is possible, just so hard to see at times. I am disgusted in my body. I hate the way I feel. I feel so fat. I am disappointed in myself that I put myself in this position to be dependent on my parents. I hate that I am exactly everything I never wanted to be! And don't want to be. I'm full of regret. I feel like I'll never reach my goals or accomplish anything in life. I know these are lies. I give them to you. I have a desire to please you, so I hope that does please you. Recovery is so much work. I never thought it would be. Help me.

So often I'm trapped in this maze of pretending and masking. I wish I could be real. Hiding behind a mask

God, why is that not enough for me? Please be enough. I only have you. I have nothing. I'm in the pit of despair. I feel like I shouldn't be. I have been here for too long. But you are leading me out…slowly, but I know that you are. I love you, I want to depend on you to meet all my needs and fill me with your love and trust you because I'm alone and miserable on my own. I'm in agony. I feel so angry at myself and depressed in my thoughts. Angry that I'm still having these thoughts. I want to be free. Help me today. I need you. I'm sorry I didn't choose a better way to cope last night. I guess I made a good decision—better than earlier. Other than the 1000 crunches and putting myself down, I used prayer and distraction by watching a movie. At least it got my mind off of the urges and I kept myself from self-injury. I still feel like my life is so screwed up and I can't seem to ever get it back on track. I am everything that I don't want to be and nothing at all the person I do want to be. I need to get things worked out, put together somehow. God, help me. I am scared and alone and I don't even know why half the time. I want to be happy. I know my energy level is higher, but I don't think my depression is all that better. Sometimes I guess—I hate myself, I feel so fat—I wanted to purge my lunch but I didn't. I did exercise but I hope you don't think I'm a failure. Help my counseling session to go well, I want to cry, I need to cry. I can't live in this numbness, it'll take over, I'll be so unhappy again. I want to serve you and not hurt myself as much as I do and not even have the desire to!

I'm supposed to work on coping skills…I was doing really good at using them. I know eventually it'll become natural but I have to concentrate on it now. I'm using journaling now, and being honest with people at my support group. I like that fact that I can see I've made progress—

Victoria pointed out that I have decreased my binge and purge episodes. I estimated I did it 20 times a week or so (at least twice a day) for a total of 60-80 times in a month, before Remuda. Then I did it 20 times in the 3-4 weeks or so after Remuda. Then once in the last 2½ weeks! That is really awesome!!! I haven't cut since I attempted suicide. I really have found that being blunt about my urges helps. I pray and tell God. I know that he knows anyways. Being honest is good. I have to keep revealing my shame.

September 29, 2006
God,

I want to over exercise. I really, really do. I know I haven't gained weight since Remuda but I feel 20 pounds heavier. I am so dissatisfied with my body, but I wish I wasn't. I thank you for bringing so many awesome people in my life. I'm so thankful for Victoria. I never have regretted a session and I can always take something helpful from it. Please continue to strengthen our therapeutic relationship, using it to help me moving forward in recovery, and maybe even touching her life in whatever way. I'm thankful for my friend "Shannon" for her love and kindness she has shown me, I pray that you will work in my life, help me to serve you. I binged and purged yesterday, and today I ate 3 balanced meals, when I didn't want to and didn't think I could do it (and didn't really want to do it at times).

September 30, 2006
God,

I SO want to cut myself. I really have been anxious and have had extremely high urges all day. I already walked today and wanted to do it again but I withheld, with your power. I almost purged when I ate a snack, but I didn't. I really want to get the intense pain out that is eating away at me. What is wrong with me? I know I exercised and probably shouldn't have done so. But to me, it was a much healthier choice than cutting. Please help me to beat this urge. I drank tea all day—I tried calling people to get out of the house…I went for a walk…I wish I could cry. I feel so alone and unhappy. Please intervene if I need it and stop me from cutting. I want to make the right choice, I really do. Amen.

Later that night…

So I gave in. I didn't resist the urges—I couldn't on my own. I wanted so badly to binge and purge so I did. I used my skills until I couldn't take it anymore. I felt they weren't working. I should have kept trying. But one I blew it—I figured, oh well! Screw it!!!!! Screw recovery!!! I want to do recovery perfectly (but obviously I can't), so when I screw up I give up because I failed and wanted to be perfect. So if I'm not perfect I may as well be 100% imperfect.

I could've called someone. I should've called someone. But I didn't. I could've done a lot of things. I even left the house. I should've let my credit card at home! Dang it. I suck.

I'm so afraid I'll wake up fat tomorrow. I just ate another cookie. I have to purge. I am so scared to eat tomorrow. I want to get back on track so I won't start this cycle, but every time I look the mirror I see such a fat, ugly girl and that causes me to hate myself more and do my behaviors. Maybe I'll exercise all night. I'm so scared. I feel like I'll never recover. I want to and think I CAN but I don't feel like it really is possible tonight. ☹

October 1, 2006
    -No urges in morning
    -Urge to throw up lunch
    -Tried to use skills-Distraction—e-mailed, watched movie, layed down and tried to nap, went for a walk, cleaned and did laundry
    -Wanted to binge
    -Ate whipped cream
    -Purged
    -Drank chocolate milk and purged
    -Ate 3 cookies (purged)
    -Ate 1 fajita (purged)
    -Left house
    -Got ice cream
    -Purged and clogged a toilet in Arabica then fled
    -Went to hang with Josh, played with Zeke, talked and laughed, hid true emotions
    -Ate 1 big cookie from Starbucks and purged
    -Ate 2 packs of Mentos and purged
    -Afraid of calories so purged in my car in a cup, then all over myself. Yuck.
The next day:
    -Wanted to get back on track and follow my meal plan
    -Healthy breakfast
    -Very anxious at lunch—cheeseburger and fries because that's what my friend had
    -Wanted to purge but didn't
    -Ate 2 pieces of pizza for dinner, chips and salsa
    -Purged
    DO I EVEN CARE!?!? Why am I so numb? I binged and purged three times this week. I'm scared...this cycle is so

hard to break. My last thought of the weekend was, "Food is gross, and throwing up feels really good."

October 5, 2006

I hate my body so much, I almost can't stand it anymore. The fact that I started my period makes me so mad. It's like I am really fat enough now to menstruate. I hate it—my worst fear is confirmed. I know it's "healthy" but I don't even care. I just want to be skinny! I seriously want to cry whenever I look in the mirror. I wish I could because I have this intense emotion flooding inside of me and I know it needs to get out eventually, but it keeps building and making me hurt so badly inside. I read online that people who attempt suicide usually don't want to die, but want the pain to stop. The pain is returning and that's what scares me. I wish I could figure out why the hell I feel so depressed and hopeless ALL the time! I want to believe it will get better but I don't. I don't believe it will. I have no hope or faith in myself. I can't stop the urges and I can't stop the behaviors. I know God can, or I'd like to believe he can, but I don't even care anymore and don't really even want to ask him. I don't feel like praying, I don't feel like reading verses about perseverance. I feel like GIVING UP! Life is too hard for me—I don't care anymore. I'm so afraid because I don't want Victoria to give up on me. I feel like she will if I tell her how I truly feel and the extent of some of the things I do. I want to cut myself! I want to hurt myself. Being on my period I've had the worst cramps and I love it—I deserve the pain (so I don't have to cut!) but I refuse to take anything. It's my fault I've gained so much weight. I hate my gross body—it's soooo fat and disgusting. My stomach is so fat, I can grab so much fat, I just want to puke thinking about it.

I need to do crunches every day to get rid of it. Yuck, Sharon you are disgusting!!! I can't feel my ribs like I used to, or my hip bones, because they are hidden under layers of gross fat! My thighs used to be half the size they are now and I used to like them but now they are huge and even though some of it is muscle I don't care—it looks so gross and disproportionate and HUGE. I need to be thin. I WANT TO BE THIN. I can't take the body I have now because I just want to hurt it. I feel like the most ungrateful person... God is so good to me and I can only focus on the negatives. I'm such a terrible person. I hate you, Sharon! I want to hurt you and make you deal with pain. You are a failure and always will be. I used to want to starve just to lose weight (3 years ago). Now I want to starve until I die! I hate that. That scares me. Why do I still have these desires! I suck. I need to tell someone. I wish I could. Maybe I can tell Victoria. I can't even touch my body and hate being touched because it reminds me of how fat I am!

October 10, 2006

I used some good skills yesterday and today even though I still have participated in behaviors. I went to the mall with Laci yesterday, got my ear pierced, called my mom, and I did Sudoku then went to bed instead of exercising all night. I might tonight, but oh well. I at least let myself sleep when I needed it. Then today after lunch with Amy (I got out of the house when I needed to), I watched "Friends." Then after dinner, I colored and did a puzzle. These seem silly to me because I feel that in my "real life" I'm not going to be able to do stupid things like that when I need to, because I'll have to work, be at school, or whatever. But, I guess I will be less stressed/anxious so often and use skills as I need to

October 19, 2006

If I really hated life, I wouldn't care so much that I feel so bad. I cut myself. It's more than the last time, but still not enough. I can't even cry. I want to. I am a disappointment: to Amy, to my parents, to God, to myself. I just want to punish myself. I wish I could purge but my throat hurts too badly. Group was depressing tonight. I found out the statistics of 15-20% of people with eating disorders dying (without treatment) but still…about 1 or 2 in 10, so that means 1 in 5 die, which are how many people were there tonight. It could be one of us, even though we've been in treatment. Who's it going to be? Treatment doesn't mean anything if your behaviors are still bad! I don't want it to be me! I have to recover. I have to stop cutting.

I just wish I had someone to hold me and love me. People criticizing every choice I make in recovery or telling me I'm doing the wrong thing DOESN'T HELP!!! It's been a week since I've purged. ☺ YAY! But…I've made it 2 ½ before so I shouldn't get excited. I'm not in enough pain. I want someone to understand me. I want someone to share my life with. I am so alone.

October 24, 2006

God is amazing! I've realized two very small but significant victories in my recovery. I've had chocolate covered pretzels—a binge food—in the house for a week. A month ago I was throwing up everything I ate. I also realized I have horrific lows after counseling. I was feeling extremely suicidal the other night but I prayed and sang, and it helped! Thoughts won't be like this forever!

October 27, 2006
God,

My week is crazy—up and down! I guess that means I'm in recovery. ☺ If I wasn't, I would continually be down. It's those few moments of success that you give me that somehow keeps me going. Thank you for giving me so much this week—I had planned on doing eating disorder behaviors again and again, but you intervened and provided ways of escape that I have taken! You AMAZE me! Thank you for Tuesday night. I have those evil, awful, consuming thoughts still, but they aren't so strong—I can combat them a lot better now. Thank you! Thank you for Wednesday night, and thinking of how bad I wanted to keep purging and hurting my body, and then I heard Victoria saying, "That's a good way to kill yourself!" And I thought, "Victoria would be sad if I killed myself." Thank you for just bringing her to my mind. Even though I knew other people care about and love me but at that moment I could only think about her and that's what I held onto.

Today (Friday) I wanted to binge and purge but you helped me. And last night, you gave me the strength to be honest with Katelyn. Thank you for her support and friendship when I've needed it most! Ripping up magazines actually helped me get anger out and I still was frustrated with my numbness to emotion—but at least I got some out. I wanted to hurt myself, yet hurt the paper. Positive destruction!

I am scared of myself, though. Not that I'll hurt myself, but that I'm ruining my life, my future, my body…and that no one will want to be with me if I have scars all over my body that I've given myself. I <u>hate</u> my body, so I cut, then I hate myself for what I did, and want to punish myself. I'm sorry for not taking better care of my body. And for loathing myself as much as I do. Cutting gives me that RELEASE because I can actually feel the pain when I do it. I can't get in touch with my emotions lately. I wish I could. Please help me, God. I feel like I'm a zombie with no feeling—being burned alive and not even caring. Help me...even if it takes until counseling tomorrow (or going twice this week). I want to feel. I love you and need you!!! Amen.

Numb

I'm tired but I can't sleep.
I'm hungry but I can't eat.
I'm lonely but I can't speak.
I'm broken but I can't heal.
I'm hurting but I can't feel.
I'm bleeding but I can't cry.
I'm failing—yet I don't care!
I need help but I'm not asking.
I'm depressed, so I isolate.
I'm afraid of what people think, so I hold back.
I am empty, so I binge and purge.
I hate myself, so I cut.
I'm ashamed, but I can't forgive myself.
I want recovery—but it's slipping out of reach.
I want to make progress but I can't focus.
I want to achieve goals but I don't have any passion.
I want to use my talents but I have no motivation.
I hate this numbness, but I have no solution.
I want to have fun, but I don't enjoy anything.
I want to love but I'm too scared.
I'm living—yet just going through the motions.
I'm dying yet I WANT TO LIVE!
I want to live...but not like this.

November 1, 2006

My thoughts just keep getting worse. I looked in the mirror last night and saw a fat girl, unattractive and disgusting. Cutting, for whatever reason appeared to be the answer, with my stupid reasoning. I didn't think about what I truly needed at the moment. I just grabbed a razor and cut. I'm destroying my body. I feel like God must hate me for doing this. How could he still love me? I'm ungrateful for everything. He keeps giving me ways of escape yet I continue hurting myself. I <u>HAVE</u> to stop! I have to be brutally honest with Victoria. Even if that means showing her, and being exposed, ashamed, and 100% honest. It's so <u>frustrating</u> that I can't feel anything. I just want to feel so badly!!! I don't feel bad, but I don't feel good...I'm just existing. This morning, I'm scared to say it—but I looked thin. I don't know if I am or not but in one glimpse I appeared to be. I don't feel pretty, I don't feel thin. I used to think hipbones were a sexy part of a woman's body. I guess I still do, that's why I cut myself there. I don't want that and I don't think any guy will find me sexy. I can't continue giving myself scars. I'm already so ugly. No one will ever love me. Why can't I be nice to myself? Maybe I can try, even if I don't believe it. Sharon—you look okay today. You are also:

Caring, encouraging, intelligent, committed, funny, creative, good listener, spontaneous, passionate (used to be), deep thinker.

I hope my feelings come back. I need to feel passion again...along with shame and guilt from what I'm doing. I'm still doing my behaviors...but in numb agony. It'll be okay. I can make it. I'm asking for help. I just have to hold on until tomorrow. Hold on to the MOMENT! I'll make it, I can do it. I can successfully conquer these urges to binge, purge, *CUT*, restrict…I know they are only going to get worse.

God, please help Victoria to understand what I feel and what I'm going through. Make tomorrow worth it. Help me to be honest even though I'm <u>SO</u> afraid. I want to cut. I want to feel. I'm so numb…I don't feel good or bad or *ANYTHING*. I'm still depressed and alone. I know I'll just be even more unsafe at home because I'll want to do things to rebel against my parents. I hurt so badly! WHY?!? Please take my self-hate, take my loathing of myself. I don't want to live like this. I want to move on with my life!!!

November 2, 2006
In the chapel after counseling:
God,

I come before you, finally seeing you more clearly for the first time in awhile. Thank you, thank you, thank you— your love and grace and hope you give me is *AMAZING!* Thank you for loving me even though I have been so far from you…doing terrible things—sinning against you and my body. I'm sorry! Please forgive me. Help me accept your love and your forgiveness. I thank you for allowing me to be quiet, to listen to what you have to say. I don't really know what to pray even now. Soaking in the quietness and presence of you is wonderful! You are so good to me, God. Where would I be without you?!? I would be dead. Or at least closer to it. This eating disorder is ruining my life! I'm miserable. You can save me. You can rescue me. You can turn my life around, and use me to my divine potential. I know you want me to commit not to self-harm. I've fallen into this for 3 months and it doesn't bring me anything good.

It only makes me unhappier. I'm sick of this. I'm sick of doing this to myself. I want to let you in. I invite you in, God. I love you! Thank you for your amazing love you have shown me! I will be victorious in this battle through your power!!!

Turning Point #755

I was weak so I rested and prayed.

I was desperate, so I asked for help.

I was alone, so I sought out people who love me.

I was hungry so I ate.

I was shameful so I exposed the secrets.

I was overwhelmed so I cried.

I was helpless so I cried out to God.

I was in awe, so I was silent.

I was sad, so I let myself feel the pain.

I was empty, so I let the love of God fill my soul.

I hated myself, so I asked God to reframe my thoughts.

I was straying away from recovery, so I admitted it and got back on track.

I was unsure of the future, so I reminded myself to be in the moment.

I was fearful of tomorrow so I trusted God with today.

I can't see my talents or gifts all the time, but I still express myself creatively.

I may feel without passion, but I am still going to live tomorrow.

I still have urges to hurt myself, but I stop and make the choice not to!

I realized I'm desperate and hopeless on my own, so I find myself at this place

of weakness and in total reliance on God, right where he wants me to be.

November 7, 2006

I'm so exhausted. I just want to sleep! I am so sick of this inbetween shit. Go one way or the other, Sharon—pick one! You give it all up, or you keep it all. Why is it such a freaking hard choice?!? I know what's better, healthier, way more rewarding than any life with a fucking eating disorder. I can't think straight, I'm sooo confused and DEPRESSED! Will this ever end?!? Will it freaking ever get better?

November 8, 2006
God,

My hope is broken. I seem to have less and less the farther I go in recovery. I am sooo disappointed in myself. I just binged and I hate myself. I feel so much worse about my body than ever. All I want to do is STARVE myself, after purging my body of any food left in it…by laxatives, throwing up—ANYTHING. ☹ I hate it. I hate me. I'm sorry!

CHAPTER 11

After many weeks of ups and downs, I became frustrated with the one person whom I looked up to the most. I was angry with Victoria, but never could understand why. It took an emotional day or two of writing, and reading a letter to her for me to uncover what I was truly feeling. I was angry that she continued to warn me of the health risks, because I knew them, and I felt stupid for still carrying out my behaviors. I was angry that she didn't seem to believe the intensity of the struggle I was still having. I was angry that she didn't say that right things or do more to help me sometimes. But I told her. This was one of the first times that I actually expressed my feelings to someone, not trying to cover them up or minimize them myself. And the funny thing was, it worked! I was honest with my ambivalence, my confusion, and my true feelings I had about recovery and myself. I expressed the deep pain I was in, and the awful thoughts I had, and the amazing thing to me was that she still liked me. She didn't yell at me, or tell me I was overreacting, or wrong. She listened. Then I believe she said, "I understand why you would feel that way," And not because that was her job as a therapist to say that, but because she really did.

*   *   *   *

November 9, 2006

Isn't it Amazing?
Isn't it amazing how I can have a whole new
outlook on life after a few minutes in prayer?
Isn't it amazing how God can restore my hope and joy
after feeling so hopeless?
Isn't it amazing how I can experience God's love and
forgiveness over and over and never quite comprehend it?
Isn't it amazing how being able to say, "I can" really
comes out of admitting, "I can't"?
Isn't it amazing how a depressing day can be turned
around if I want it to be?
Isn't it amazing how God can transform my thinking
if I just ask?
Isn't it amazing how God provides exactly what I need
when I need it?
Isn't it amazing to sit and be at peace with life even
when things seem to be falling apart?
Isn't it amazing how in a fallen, dark world I can wake
up and be grateful for another day in this
crazy thing called life?

November 12, 2006
God,

Why do I continue to hate myself!?! More than ever. All I want to do is eat. And all I want to do is starve. Or at least lose weight. So I binge and purge, then starve for days. I feel like I've done my part today as far as staying in recovery. But I still feel like I ate too much. I hate this and I don't know when it'll end. I hate the intensity of my feelings. I want to hurt myself! Sooooo badly! I want to grab a razor and destroy every part of my body that I despise—punishing it for getting so fat. I hate it. I hate myself. I feel so disgusting in my body. I feel such pain and regret and overall confusion. I want to starve the rest of the week. I don't know if I want to commit to recovery anymore.

November 14, 2006

I can't even put my feelings down on paper. They are so strong, I feel like I could seriously hurt myself if I wanted to. I just want to hurt my body because I have such an intense hatred towards it. I hate it. I hate how I look—I look DISGUSTING! I am so fat, I HATE IT!!!!! I can feel and see the fat—it's so obvious and so gross. I'm so sad. ☹ I wonder if it's ever going to go away (the depression, and fat...). I almost can't even look at my body without crying. I want to cut because I hate my body, and I hate my body so I cut...I want to cut soooo badly! But I'm trying to positively cope. I seem to be okay for a few days at the beginning of the week, and then it gets harder but I still try, then by the weekend I just CRASH. I know what I have to do tomorrow to get back on track but I don't know what I'm gonna do. I just want to starve until I lose a few pounds. I am so disappointed in myself, my worst fear it coming true—that

I would gain all this weight back and I have. I'm such a failure!!! I hate myself. I know recovery meant restoring weight but it doesn't mean to keep gaining like this!

November 15, 2006

So, I got off the phone with Victoria and binged and purged. Out of rebellion... out of anger and disappointment, and just because I already had my mind set on it and couldn't admit it out loud. Once again I hold everything to such a high expectation... that my new antidepressants will make me feel better right away, that my friends won't let me down, that I'll be perfect at recovery, and that my therapist will give me better advice than, "Go to a movie." Sadly, if I had taken her advice—I probably wouldn't have had such a bad relapse tonight. I have the expectation of everyone else fixing my problems. And that's not happening (and it's not going to happen).

The high is gone now and I feel like shit. I want to do it again but I'm not going to (tonight anyway). I actually have some energy and don't want to go to bed right now. I still hate my body so much—the change is insane that I notice with myself. I cried hysterically earlier before I binged and purged because I couldn't stand the image I saw in the mirror. I wanted to be close to people last week—now I'm so embarrassed and ashamed of my body that I don't want anyone to touch it, I don't want anyone to see it, or even be near it. I HATE IT!!!! Ahhhh I don't know how I look, but I think it's HUGE and disproportionate and UGLY and FAT!!! And sooo not muscular and thin like I used to be. I hate my body, I hate it!!! I am gonna cut. I don't even care. I might as well give myself scars because I'm freaking ugly and fat anyways. I'm so ungrateful. Sharon you suck! I hate myself. Why can't I be thankful for my body and tolerate it?!? ☹ God, I'm sorry. I wish I had a guy who would appreciate me and my body and tell me I'm beautiful and love me for who I am.

I felt so out of control today. I wanted to hurt myself, and tried. I purged about 30 times then went to work out. I should have taken more laxatives. I wanted to pass out, I didn't care. The words of a roommate at Remuda are repeating in my head, "Tell someone whenever you want to hurt yourself. No matter what, tell someone. ALWAYS!" Should I tell? Who should I tell? When? AHH!!! I didn't try to kill myself. I did try to hurt myself.

God I need a friend RIGHT now!!!! PLEASE send me someone at this moment!!! I tried calling Katelyn, Ashley, Amy, and Lane but they didn't answer. I feel so alone. I need help. I can keep writing—keep praying. I know that you'll help me—you always do. I just have to keep writing the rest of this page. I can do it, I trust you. God, thank you for this week—even in my failures, I have learned so much. Maybe I needed a break from counseling for a reason, for time to think and listen to you and not have someone else directing my thoughts. I've done so much wrong. Please forgive me. I've hurt you. I've hurt myself. I need you!!! I often try to convince myself that I don't but I SO do! Take my pain, take my frustration, take my doubt! Take my self-hate, take my self-harm, take my purging, take my binging, take my over exercising, take my starving! Take my depression, take my hopelessness! ☹ I don't know why I feel like this but I do. I just want to scream. And cry. Thank you for letting my feel my emotions again. Please be with me! I love you. Amen.

His magnificent love
His infinite grace
holds me close
when i'm afraid
of letting go
and trusting.
He sees beyond me
and my life, my efforts
and my failures.
there is hope.
even in the blackness
even in the lowest valley.
when i'm desperate
and alone
and helpless.
there's a voice
calling my name
and i answer
through the tears
and the pain and the frustration
of not being able to see Him
and fearful of the future
and the next step.
i cried today
for the first time
not out of anger or depression
but out of complete awe
and admiration
of my amazing God.
Why is the fear of getting better actually harder to face
than the fear of never recovering?

CHAPTER 12

I was frustrated in my ambivalence in recovery. I desperately wanted it one day, and then absolutely wanted my eating disorder the next. I didn't understand myself, until I came across the book, *I Hate You, Don't Leave Me* one day in Borders. As I read, I realized that I was manipulating everyone around me, wanting them to give up on me, so I would have an excuse to give up on myself. I needed confirmation from everyone, and was afraid to give up, in fear that I would let everyone down and disappoint them with my failure. But if I could wait for Victoria to give up on me, by telling her every week how bad I was, then I would know everyone figured I was hopeless, and I wouldn't have to try at recovery anymore. I was playing games with everyone around me, testing them to see if they were still in it with me for the long run.

By reading this book, about Borderline Personality Disorder, I related to so much of it. My indecisiveness,

I'm unproductive but I want to have energy
I hate people but I love them
I'm indecisive obviously
I'm hopeless but I have a little hope left
I love my eating disorder but I freaking hate it!
It has ruined my life!

2 Corinthians 4:8-9 "We are hard pressed on every side,
but not crushed; perplexed but not in despair; persecuted but
not abandoned; struck down, but NOT DESTROYED!"

November 23, 2006
5:10 a.m.
Sharon—God doesn't want you to do this to yourself!!!
I made a bad decision last night. Maybe I thought I was
"recovered" enough to slack off. All the counseling in the
world won't help. I have the insight, and I know what I have
to do. I can't go back there and just say I don't know why I'm
doing this. I can't blame the treatment, or my support team.
I have to do the right things—every decision—YES or NO!
I need to get back on track. I can't do this to myself. I can't
live like this.
My behaviors today:
-Restricted all day
-Binged on cookies, M&M's, salad, milkshake
-Purged forever
-Took laxatives
-Cut my stomach…a new area. ☹ I didn't think I
cut it very bad but I did, not really bad, but worse than I
intended…scary.
-Cut my hipbones ☹

220

-A series of self-punishment

Relapsing was uncomfortable tonight. Not safe and normal like before. Recovery used to seem foreign. Now it really doesn't! My recovery can be a comedy or a tragedy, it is up to me.

November 24, 2006

Why am I doing really, really well, or NOT GOOD AT ALL??? This sucks! It's crappy. I just wish I could get it together because I look so gross! I hate my body. ☹ I wish I could just eat right—and enjoy food. I guess I should concentrate on being healthy and striving towards that rather than not caring. I want to do the right thing. But every time I relapse it's worse and worse. I'll do so many things and not even care, while before I would feel awful. Now I binge and purge and don't even really care. I went to 4 grocery stores today. 4!?!? I'm insane. I got one thing at each and half binged then purged, then threw the rest away because I was so disgusted with it and myself. I feel so gross but I have no motivation to eat dinner or get back on track tomorrow. I wish I did. AHHH! I want to be alone yet I want to be with people. I'm so torn again! I hate it because every time my behaviors seem not as bad. If I binge and purge, cut, then take laxatives and starve the next day, I'm happy if I simply binge, purge, and cut the next day. When that is still really bad. And it's not like I'm trading one behavior for another (with the laxatives and cutting). I'm adding!!!! AHHHH!!! Life is so frustrating!!! I AM A FREAKING FAILURE!!!!!!!!!!!!!!!!!!!!!!

November 26, 2006

I want to recover. I hate this. I'm sick of puking 20 times every day. It's normal to me, but I realize it's not normal. I worked 7 hours today, then binged and purged for about 4 hours total. How pathetic. Plus all I ate all day was carrots and diet pop. I'm stuck. I've been stuck for a week and a half. Tomorrow can be a good day. It can be, after I finish being sick from all the laxatives. I want all the food out of me. I love that feeling. Of being empty. Of being free from calories that make me fat. I feel really hypocritical. But I can't help it, it's how I feel. I like it. I used to not want to give up my eating disorder and hated it. Now I want to give it up but I like it. Back and forth. This shit is killing me.

It felt good destroying the picture I drew of a sexy woman in a bikini. I was proud of it, like I am with my body sometimes, but I hurt so badly inside because I hate myself, and so I destroy my body. Then I went crazy with cutting her, as I also do with myself. I have to stop before I hurt myself. I kept myself from doing it tonight. It IS possible!!!!

*   *   *   *

From the depth of a relapse, I felt absolutely hopeless. But my feelings passed, a week or so later, and I was renewed with hope and excitement for recovery once again. The more and more I got my feelings out through artwork, prayer and poetry, the better I began to feel. This poem was how the title to the book was born:

November 29, 2006

> *I thought it might be fun to diet.*
> *I am disgusted with my body, still.*
> *I thought it was smart to purge everything I ate.*
> *It became an extremely dangerous addiction.*
> *I thought I needed to starve.*
> *It's harder to start eating again every time.*
> *I thought exercise was the way to do it.*
> *It became an obsession.*
> *I thought laxatives would give me instant relief.*
> *They did but it was never enough.*
> *I thought cutting would ease the pain.*
> *It did, only for a little bit, and now I'm scarred.*
> *I'm in this cycle, and I feel hopeless.*
> *I continue to fail.*
> *But I have a choice every day.*
> *Every moment.*
> *I know what to do.*
> *I'm gonna do it.*
> *I'm going to freaking DO IT!!!!*
> *I'm gonna freaking recover!!!!*

I'm not going to live with an eating disorder. It isn't living. I'm not going to die over a toilet. And I'm not going to live with my head over it either! I'm better than that. There is more to life for me. THERE IS HOPE!!!!!

December 6, 2006

I feel like I deserve this pain. Punishment for what I've done. I hate myself so much! I freaking can't do anything. I feel absolutely worthless and I want to DESTROY my body!!!! I have in some ways. I ate so much....about 3000 calories, and then I purged it all. Then I hated myself and felt so fat and gross and disgusting. SO I CUT! It also relieved the pain inside—the suicidal thoughts. Then I kept going—my hips, my stomach, my legs. I couldn't stop. I didn't want to either. I cried hysterically. I felt out of control. I WAS out of control. I wanted to die because I can't live with this pain. Physical pain feels so much better. It actually calms me.

I bled so much, it gets worse every time. I just watched it drip down, I watched my hand covered in my own puke. I deserve it. It describes me. Worthless, disgusting, nothing. I don't know why I cut if I don't even tell anyone. No one sees it. If it's a cry for help it's a stupid way to do it.

Caught in a fucking battle
I hate this
I want to be alive and free
But I keep falling down
Farther and farther
I want to die
Cutting is the only thing
That makes me feel better
Food is gross
Purging is only somewhat relieving
I want to cut my body
Not because it's not thin
But because I hate myself
And I'm hurting inside
And I feel hopeless about living
And don't care about tomorrow
I'm a mess, a complete mess
And the worst part is…
I've done this to myself.

Later the same night…

I feel so disconnected from my body and myself. I looked in the mirror and stared into my own eyes. It's not me. I saw my body and how much I had cut. It's getting out of control. I'm scared. I don't know if I'll ever be normal. Or better. I FEEL HOPELESS. Last time I felt like this—I wanted to live. I CHOSE TO! I can still choose tonight. As long as I make it through tonight. What's done is done. <u>I stopped.</u> God,

By your power, I stopped binging and purging and cutting. I could've gone on. But I didn't. I just need to hold on. Help me hold on until tomorrow!

December 7, 2006

I'm scared to recover
I'm tired of this game
I want it yet I hate it
Every day is the same
I end up in a relapse
Resorting to my destruction
I binge and purge and cut myself
I'm falling apart and can hardly function
Why can't I just stay on track?
I keep on screwing up
I have a desire to get well
But evil suicidal thoughts interrupt
My passion that was so strong
Just the other day
Is lost and broken and hopelessness
Has carried it away
Dirty, alone, and shameful
For how I think and what I do

I've hurt myself, I wish I could
Be honest and be true
Please O God—hear my cry
Help me hold on as I wait
Save me, rescue me from this hell
Before it is too late

December 13, 2006
It happened AGAIN
I couldn't STOP
All I wanted was instant relief
Hurting myself to numb the pain
The pain that I can't describe,
Can't understand,
As much as I try
It always comes back
More intense
So it takes more…
more food
more purging
more pills
more cutting
and
less crying
less fear
less shame
I'm screwed.
Maybe I want this
Because I love it so much
And I can't really even
Remember my life without it
The glimpse I had of recovery

Is gone—SO far gone
Buried under so much self-harm
And self-HATE
I don't even know why
But I need help!
I WANT OUT!
I wondered if my feelings are real.
They are.
I can feel again.
But only because I see my blood and the cuts on my ugly
body.
The damage that I've done to the outside reflects the
inward pain.
What do I want?
What should I do?
Everything inside my mind is
SCREAMING to give in.
I feel better…
Only because I cut myself.

January 10, 2007
Every time I cut myself, I care a little bit less.
It's not an option for me to continue living like this.
I've tried to kill myself with my eating disorder,
Rather than just lose weight.
I'm full of regret.
I've let everyone down.
I'm lost and abandoned.
Or maybe it's me who has abandoned God.
A God I never really knew
Because I thought he demanded perfection
And performance and an ongoing

Happy-go-lucky relationship with him
That was easy.
But I found it to be a struggle—
Extremely difficult,
Constantly pleasing those around me.
But I was never good enough.
Then I slipped and fell
Into a love affair with an eating disorder
And gave up on God.
I thought it would fill this void inside me,
And it did—for a while.
Now I'm miserable, alone, confused.
I'm drowning in hopelessness.
Suicide seems like the only answer.
Sometimes when I purge, I pray that it will be
The last time!
Maybe I'll starve, punishing myself for all I've screwed up,
And all I've let go.

CHAPTER 13

Recovery went up and down, but most importantly, I lived through it all. I had six horrific months identical to my life before treatment. Well, almost identical. The behaviors were still there, not eating for days, purging everything for weeks, and the urges to cut were unbearable at times. But every once in a while, with the power of Christ, I found his perfect way of escape. Two days of starving didn't turn into seven. A night of binging and purging didn't end with the ultimate punishment of cutting. My depressing poems and artwork were a time for me to process my emotions and actually get them out. I developed my own coping skills. To an outsider, I probably wouldn't have looked like I was making any progress. But I knew God was rescuing me, and teaching me, every day, through every stumble and victory. And slowly, things began to go a little differently. Once again, I chose to be honest at counseling, not minimizing my problems because I knew that wouldn't help. And I took charge of my recovery, and my counseling sessions, speaking up for what I wanted and needed, from Victoria, but most of all, finally asking God to fulfill my needs. In February, after a week of ruminating thoughts of cutting, the obsession was tearing me apart. I actually did not give in the urges, instead literally taking it out on paper multiple times a day. I got a tattoo on my wrist of the reference 1 Corinthians 6:19, and would meditate on it when I knew I couldn't fight the urges alone. I hated myself for having such evil thoughts that wouldn't go away. I didn't think I could take it another day. But I knew what I needed to do that weekend at counseling. Victoria and I went up to the chapel after our session and prayed together. In the silence, in the sunlit room, we were both overwhelmed with the presence of God. I prayed for deliverance from my thoughts, and for the first time, realized that I absolutely could not recover on my own no matter how hard I tried.

*   *   *   *

February 13, 2007
God,

I felt hopeless last night. I still am. I had to draw disgusting pictures of myself just to get out the cutting urges. But I destroyed them. Maybe that's bad, how I want to destroy my body. Please help me. I don't want to hurt my body. I need to get it out though and tell someone. PLEASE let there be an opening with Victoria this week. I know I don't need her but I do need to process these terrible thoughts and urges with someone. Please God, may there be an opening today or tomorrow. I don't want to call her but I don't want to cut myself either. I feel so guilty and terrible for having these thoughts. I don't have a plan to kill myself but I want to. If I decided to, I would cut myself how I described last night. I want to tell someone before it's too late. I know the only person I could possibly reveal this to is Victoria. I have faith that you can make this possible. I'm so alone, and scared about my thoughts. You are so awesome, God, you have provided so much. Thank you for what you have given me. I trust you, Lord. Provide what I need. I'm sad. I'm scared. I'm alone. I'm empty. I still hurt so much inside. Fill me. I need YOU. Please give me the help I need before I give up. Amen.

February 19, 2007

I'm dying more each day. Every time I cut another part of my body, or purge more and more, I am giving part of myself up. What will I do when nothing is left?

February 21, 2007

I am such an incredible failure. Since Saturday I haven't even cared or wanted to stop what I've been doing. Saturday I cut and purged everything I ate. I even ate a healthy lunch and thought I was okay, but was I??? NO! I am an idiot and went home and purged it all. Then I cut myself again…it's so addicting. I loved it. I'm so screwed up.

Then my depression only worsened. Sunday I stayed home and purged everything I ate ONCE again! And then I cut again because I wanted and deserved intense punishment and pain. If I can't understand the internal pain at least I can see and understand the physical pain. I HATE myself!

I cried. But I cleaned myself up, stopped the bleeding and tried to confess it. Sometimes I feel so hopeless about it, I like it. I am SICK and I can't imagine not doing it anymore. God please change me. I've tried forever to change myself. I can't. I never will. You are strong and mighty, and I am not.

Yesterday I was an absolute failure. I binged out of control and PURGED until I was empty of nasty calories. I wanted to cut but I made it through that urge. I'm still HOPELESS. I have such good days or hours, and then I crash and have a low, then punish myself for it!

But, there is a God! ☺ He provided an opening at counseling this weekend. I hope I can hold on until then. I'm weak and don't even want to go on. Just survive today.

Psalm 94:18-19 "When I said, 'My foot is slipping,' your love, O Lord, supported me. When anxiety was great within me, you consolation brought joy to my soul."

February 27, 2007
God,

I love you! I love you! Thank you so much for loving me and most of all, for showing me so evidently these past few days. Thank you for the session I had on Saturday, the intensity was amazing, your presence was so clear to me. I praise you for the insight you have been giving me, and most of all—the HOPE! I finally see you, God. I want to give my recovery to you.

Thank you for the quietness in the chapel, for the stillness, the comfort, and the peace that overwhelmed me. I long to bask in your presence. I want to bring you glory!

Please, guard my thoughts! Fight for me God, give me the strength for tomorrow. Amen.

February 28. 2007
God,

It's early and I'm tired. But you have given me a motivation and HOPE that I haven't had in such a long time. I pray that you would be everything to me today. I am in need. I know I will struggle with food today. I want to restrict. But I ask that you will help this desire to go away. I know that pleasing you means not hurting my body. I admit, I still love my eating disorder. It is always there for me. I love the feelings and relief that it brings. I have a desire to keep living in it. But I know you can take it away. I long for and await the day I will not worry so much about food. And I believe it will come in the near future. Help me to stop and think before I hurt myself. Give me a clear mind, so that I can remember 1 Corinthians 6:19, that my body is a temple. Please give me the strength to say no to the urges that attack me constantly. I love you, Lord. I give this day to you. Amen.

"Faithfulness...not success." -Mother Theresa

March 2, 2007

I think a major turning point in my recovery has been the realization that the lies from Satan started as, "Cutting feels good," or "Throwing up in the answer...you don't need to eat." And it is true that it does feel good. I know I can pray for God to take that feeling away, but it honestly still feels good to me. God knows, he made our bodies. Instead, as I have recently been overwhelmed with the opposite, I see that my entire beliefs are invalid. Satan tells me that I DESERVE the pain, that I AM worthless, that I'm never going to be loved or forgiven, that I deserve to die...and that is NEVER true. Now, I tell God how I feel and ask him to defeat these lies, and to speak his truth to me—that I am loved, I am forgiven, I am his child, I am of great worth, I am redeemed, I am with hope, and I am complete. I have been asking him to change my thoughts, and he totally is!

Also, I've been told that I should recover for myself, or for my family and friends. But I fully believe now I should recover for God! Isn't life all about him anyway? If I'm just doing it for me, I'm still the focus, not God. And if I "recover" I take all the credit and think I have done something amazing on my own.

March 4, 2007

I'm growing so much, and becoming less scared of recovery. I am becoming my own person. I'm developing my own passions, values, personality, and making my own decisions. The more I think for myself, the more I am empowered. I am realizing it's okay to be myself, that it's okay and even vital to be open in relationships, and allow others to see the real me. I'm learning it doesn't matter if you have a tattoo (which, as a rebellious Amish girl, I do), or dress stylish or wear make-up or not. People are beautiful for who they are.

I feel as if this past year has been a blessing. All the pain has made me into a completely different person. It's like I almost had to be ripped away from my old self to actually have this insight and new perspective on God and life. I feel so much more in love with God, closer than I ever was, when I was lost in legalism. I had to break away from it to see clearly. I'm so glad I've finally found my life; a life that is truly fabulous with God.

John 10:10 "I have come that they may have life, and have it to the full."

CHAPTER 14

My thoughts and ultimately my life began to transform. My eating disorder was becoming less a part of my life. I still struggled with restricting and purging, but it was less intense and less frequent. I still struggled with anxiety, as I was refraining from my eating disorder to deal with those emotions. And I still had overwhelming urges to end my life. But none of these things led to a downward spiral that I couldn't seem to pull myself out of for months. I began to trust less in my own self-control, and gave my weakness over to God. And I even began to give myself a little bit of grace when I made a mistake instead of punishing myself, remembering that God did not think I was a failure, and still loved me abundantly.

I actually became in tune with myself, and had a realistic view on my recovery. I was able to become an independent woman in the world, becoming more and more confident in, and okay with the person I truly was. Positive thoughts gradually outweighed the negatives. I actually made a list of 63 ways (and still counting…) that I had improved in that month. Just to name a few:

- ❖ *I'm not having such obsessive thoughts.*
- ❖ *Eating small meals regularly (and not purging!).*
- ❖ *Going to God for deliverance from suicidal thoughts, and my desires for my eating disorder.*
- ❖ *I'm letting myself sleep, and cry.*
- ❖ *Praying with friends.*
- ❖ *Seeking out spiritual guidance on my own.*
- ❖ *Finding a new job that was challenging, but something I can handle.*
- ❖ *Making friends at school*
- ❖ *Calling or going to someone's house in time of crisis.*
- ❖ *Doing more artwork and journaling again, rather than suppressing my emotions.*
- ❖ *Getting the help I need, rather than doing what others want me to do, just to please them.*
- ❖ *Taking time for myself.*
- ❖ *Having passion and actively pursuing my dream to become an art therapist.*

As I continued moving forward and dealing with my intense urges, emotions and mistakes on my own, God laid it on my heart one night that I no longer needed counseling as much. I was surprised, because I actually was okay with it. In the past, I could never imagine a week without Victoria…sometimes I couldn't even make it that long, counting down the days until my next session. I figured I would go to see her as long as possible, until she kicked me out. However, I was becoming more mature, and I was glad that the decision to cut back on counseling was my own. God brought it to my mind when I least expected it, but was completely ready. It wasn't easy. I was nervous and couldn't sleep the night before I would tell Victoria. But I didn't chicken out, and I didn't change my mind based on others' opinions. I also didn't make an impulsive decision such as never going back to counseling ever, like I would have done in the past. I did what I needed to do to continue moving forward in recovery.

*   *   *   *

March 9, 2007
God,

Please hear my cry tonight. I am in desperate need. Psalm 86:1 "Hear, O Lord, and answer me, for I am poor and needy." I am so confused now, but at the same time, I feel your peace. I want to lift up tomorrow's session with Victoria to you. In her quiet office, be present. Let us be overwhelmed by you, by your peace, by your love, and by your guidance you will give us. Please allow the perfect number of minutes for us. Please give both of us wisdom, and that we will know, with absolutely no doubt in our minds, what is best. I know you did not lay this desire on my heart for no reason. I am committing all of recovery to you, and that means counseling as well. I have to trust you, God! I can't keep holding onto what I want. Trusting you with everything means even being willing to give up that which is the hardest. I can't hold onto counseling, or to Victoria, as wonderful as she is, if you have better things for me right now. I'm not going to miss purging, I'm not going to miss starving, at least not as much as I will miss Victoria. And maybe, that bond between us is holding me back. I don't know, God. I don't know. But I know you know. I'm scared, but I place tomorrow in your hands. Be with Victoria, speak to her, even now and tomorrow morning. We need you, God. Help us to see what is best for me, for both of us, even though it may be hard to understand or accept. You give and take away, God, but you make everything beautiful in its time (Ecclesiastes 3:10). Please make tomorrow wonderful... how great are YOU God! Through it all, may ALL see how great you are!!!! Amen.

Ecclesiastes 3:1 "For there is a time for everything and a season for everything under the earth."

March 12, 2007
God,

I come before you with so much gratitude. You are so amazing. Today I feel like giving up. I want to starve. I want to purge. I even want to die. I'm scared that the worst is coming back. But I can't live in fear. I don't expect every day to be perfect. They won't be, for sure! You have blessed me so much, with bringing new people into my life, by providing a job, taking care of me financially and physically, and by the revelation of my artistic ability. That has helped me so much in dealing with emotions, and has become an expression of worship to you. You have met my every need, and assured me with Christ's words, that "Your Father knows what you need before you ask him" (Matthew 6:8). Your hand was with Stacy as she called my mom. You hand led me to Victoria. You knew I needed treatment at Remuda specifically, and provided me with loving parents to make it happen. And you have given me so much encouragement, support, love and HOPE through this entire journey.

I want to give up sometimes, God. But I know you have brought me sooo far. Only by your power alone could I have just eaten lunch and kept it down. I'm still struggling mentally. I still have such strong urges to end my life. I immediately want to give up when life is hard and overwhelming. Please God, continue to remind me that life is worth living! Especially when I am depressed and think I have no way out. I trust you God—you will make my life more and more joyful and GLORIOUS to you! What would I do without you? I have no idea.

Conclusion

I have asked people how they have recovered. Some give a textbook answer; they went through an entire outpatient program and did everything recommended, or that they saw a counselor, dietician, and attended a support group. A friend of mine was hospitalized for a couple of weeks while struggling with anorexia, and then decided to eat again because she was threatened to be sent to the psych ward. Or some have said it was "just a phase," they went through, but I can tell they are still obsessed with exercise, dieting, and their bodies. Nothing like that led to my personal recovery. I have always done things a little unorthodox, but I am glad I can say I am not recovering by following a rigid meal plan and weekly counseling, dietician appointments, and support group after support group. I tried all that. And of course I failed. Going against the system actually worked for me. I learned how to express my needs, and find a way to get them met rather than waiting around, or following a system because I was "supposed to." Instead of letting others control my recovery, I took control of it and made it my own. I was honest with what I needed, and as I moved forward in recovery, God revealed to me what was best. Nothing can force someone to get better. But there are so many ways God can lead those struggling, with absolutely *any difficulty*, to freedom.

I truly began making the most progress in recovery on an ordinary snowy Ohio day, while walking back to my apartment from class. I realized that I had sat through class (a statistics class nonetheless), and didn't calculate the number of calories I had eaten that day. I didn't dwell on the fact that I had eaten breakfast, or call myself a failure for giving into food for energy. I was simply walking home, and I wasn't thinking about food, until I realized I wasn't thinking about food, my empty apartment, or what I would binge and purge when I arrived there.

One of my favorite movies is *Stranger than Fiction*. After discovering that he is going to die, Harold Crick (Will Ferrell) takes a chance, and gives up his safe, solitary lifestyle, which has kept him from doing things he always wanted to do. He gave up his obsessive compulsiveness, tapped into his talent—music, and was open to a relationship. The most relevant part of the movie to my recovery is the quote, "Harold no longer counted brush strokes, he no longer ate alone...instead, Harold did that which terrified him before, that which the unrelenting lyrics of numerous punk rock songs told him to do. Harold Crick lived his life."

So I too decided to live my life. One morning, after a time of starving, I eyed a plate of my roommate's chocolate chip cookies. I had denied myself them all week, and I finally realized that since I wanted to eat a cookie, I would take a chance and let myself. So I did. I had two. For breakfast. Without purging. And then I forgot about it until lunch. It wasn't following a meal plan, it was actually pretty unhealthy if you're following the food pyramid. But it was so significant. I took a chance and threw out my "safe" breakfast and diet foods I had planned on eating all day, and ate something I hadn't allowed myself to enjoy in so long. Maybe since the fall of '03. It was then, ironically, chocolate chip cookies were the start of my actual struggle with purging. That was the first enticement of an eating disorder, which led to this struggle and obsession, which without God's grace, would have destroyed me. I guess you could say that my eating disorder began, and ended with chocolate chip cookies.

*   *   *   *

So I conclude this journey from despair, to absolute hopelessness, to glimpses of hope, and finally, emerging from the grasp of evil—constantly learning more through triumphs, slips and falls, but most importantly, by being held in the hand of God. He was by my side all along. I just was too enwrapped in the chaos I had created and the darkness that surrounded me to see right in front of my face. I didn't always want his help, but he was there the whole time, waiting patiently, loving me and hurting for me desperately.

How does one recover from an addiction? From bondage in sin? From evil thoughts and deep, continual depression? I can only offer this one bit of advice packed full of truth—God alone is perfect. I have found such freedom and comfort in that, knowing I can't do it alone but there is hope in Christ! We all make mistakes. It doesn't mean we are failures. God is overflowing with love and forgiveness, and in his perfection, can rescue us from that which seems impossible.

"And we, who with unveiled faces all reflect the Lord's glory, are being transformed into his likeness with ever-increasing glory…" 2 Corinthians 3:18